ESSENTIAL TRUTH

*A Practical, Biblical Look
at the Christian Life*

J. Cliff Canipe

Essential Truth
A Practical, Biblical Look at the Christian Life

All Scripture quotations taken from the New American Standard Bible®
(NASB), Copyright © 1960, 1962, 1963, 1968, 1971, 1972, 1973, 1975,
1977, 1995 by The Lockman Foundation.
Used by permission. www.lockman.org.

All italics used in Scripture quotations are added by the author.

Published by Equippers International
P.O. Box 126002
Benbrook, TX 76126

ISBN: 978-0-578-71280-2
eISBN: 978-0-578-71684-8
LCCN: 2020911178

Printed in the United States of America
First Edition 2020

To Stephanie, Camille, Natalie, and Wesley, for your relentless patience and love for me as a husband and a father.

The journey together has been amazing!

Acknowledgments

One of the greatest joys in life is found in sharing it with other people. I am always amazed at how God brings the right people into our lives at the right time. So many people have played a vital role in my own personal journey. Thank you to Ken, John, Mike, and Gene, who were there for me in my first formative years as a believer. Thank you to all those who were instrumental in my discovering a deeper life with the Spirit in a time when my soul longed for more. Thank you to the professors who imparted their wisdom and knowledge to me during my academic studies.

Thank you to DeVern Fromke, whose book—*No Other Foundation*—appeared in the most unlikely and unexpected country and shook me in the deepest places. To others, including E. Earle Ellis, T. Austin Sparks, Watchman Nee, Dan Stone & David Gregory, and James Fowler, thank you all for your sacrifice to know the Lord and to share with others the One you have found. All of these men have deeply impacted my journey, helped to shape my beliefs, and given me words at the perfect time for what my spirit was seeing. Some I have met personally. For the ones I have not, I will one day in heaven, and I am sure the fellowship will be sweet.

Thank you to Rene Brown and Jack Horn, two very humble, elder pilgrims who have modeled for me what it means to love Jesus with all your heart and to hunger deeply for the truth that is only mined through hours of prayer, discussions, debates, and many cups of tea. You have taught me that you are never too old to learn!

Thank you to my family who has always supported me to pursue the Lord at all costs, which sometimes demanded of them what they may not have been ready or willing to give themselves. Your sacrifices are a fragrant aroma before the Lord.

Lastly, I want to acknowledge the one person in my life who is always my greatest inspiration. Thank you, Stephanie—my amazing wife—for your never-ending support and encouragement to pursue Jesus more. Thank you for the endless discussions (and debates) we have had over the years, and your willingness to engage me at the deepest level of beliefs and convictions. Thank you for your critical and valuable editing skills. I greatly respect your personal walk with Jesus and your understanding and knowledge of the Scriptures. You are my Barnabas in every way—my encourager and my crown.

Endorsements

Essential Truth is one of the clearest presentations of everything God has freely given us in Christ that I have ever read—and I myself have been writing about these truths for 25 years. Cliff Canipe provides not only superb biblical teaching, but also weaves in priceless how-to's of truly walking by faith in Christ in us. To anyone who wonders if there is more to the Christian life than trying hard in your own effort yet never quite measuring up, here is your answer! I was hugely blessed by the book, and I could not recommend it more highly.

David Gregory
Author of *The New York Times'* bestseller
Dinner with a Perfect Stranger and
The Rest of the Gospel: When the Partial Gospel Has Worn You Out

I have come to know Cliff not only as a passionate expositor of the truths of the gospel, but also as a faithful and dear friend. Everything that he teaches is also a lived reality. I am thankful that he has come to a point where he could share his insight and experience of the New Covenant in this manner. This book addresses some of the most essential gospel truths of the Christian life. Each topic is addressed in an accessible yet profound and liberating way. This is not the kind of book that you can read lightly, but it is the kind of book that you cannot wait to share with others.

Philip Du Toit, PhD
Senior Lecturer of New Testament
North-West University, South Africa

I have known Cliff since 1993, and he has become one of my closest friends in life. We have laughed together, cried together, prayed together, traveled together, and ministered together. He is tireless in his pursuit of Christ, the truth of the gospel, a New Testament interpretation of the kingdom of God, and the truth of the word of God. This book is inspirational, foundational, educational, exegetical, exact, precise, full of insight—both spiritual and practical—challenging, and even confrontational in the best possible way. I recommend him and his book highly!

Rick Montgomery
Director, ZEB'S Foundation
Texas, United States

For those who have a longing in their spirit for something more than what they see in the church as they know it or were taught it, Dr. Canipe's book will open up entirely new vistas. Each of the chapters opens a subject crucial to our walk in the Lord Jesus Christ. From these vital tidbits of truth, many will be inspired to dig deeper in the faith as they come to know their Lord in wonderful new ways.

Rene P. Brown
Foundation Ministries International
Texas, United States

We are the generation with the greatest access to Christian information, content, preaching, books, messages, and teachings that has ever existed in human history. However, in view of the blunt reality of great immaturity and lack of practical responses from the Church to the main emotional, physical, and spiritual problems of society, I can say that our generation needs desperately to be based on Christ more than ever. We need the *Essential Truth* for the transformation we dream of to take place. More than ever, we need to turn to the biblical foundations that generate a practical attitude of personal transformation and positively affect all areas of our lives and society as a whole. Each chapter of this book is an invitation to a practical life of faith and maturity in Christ. It is the type of reading that removes the weight of religiosity, communicating Christian fundamentals in a simple and objective way. More than recommending this book, I mainly recommend Cliff's life, family, and ministry, as I know of his love and zeal for the gospel. I am extremely honored to read and endorse my friend's labor of faith and obedience.

Hiago Angelucci
Training Director, University of the Nations
Curitiba, Brazil

There are many people writing books these days. You don't have to be a person of character or even be a passionate follower of Jesus to write a "Christian" book, but it helps. Cliff is the real deal. He loves Jesus, his family, and his neighbors. Cliff is also a brilliant and gifted writer. It has taken Cliff a lifetime to live this book. Buy it. Read it. Apply it to your life. You will be encouraged to love Jesus and your neighbors too.

Richard Henderson
Founder, Fellowship of the Sword
Texas, United States

CONTENTS

PREFACE

Why write a book about the Christian life? Obviously there have already been plenty of books written on the topic. "Why?" is a question I have asked myself many times over the years. I guess it is a question that every author must ask before writing a book. The last thing I want to do is to repeat what others have already said. But this is virtually inevitable. The writer of Ecclesiastes told us that there was nothing new under the sun (Eccl. 1:9). I don't want to be so presumptuous to think I have something new to say that has never been said before.

Throughout the years I have been challenged and stimulated by various people through their own writings and personal journeys with the Lord. I mentioned some of these in the acknowledgments above. But there must be a more viable reason for writing a book than to merely summarize and present the thoughts of others. I think I have finally found that reason.

I am compelled to share what I have experienced and how it has impacted my life and my walk with the Lord over the last thirty-four years. I would not say that everything in this book is *the* absolute truth, but I am confident that it does contain much truth. With that conviction, I offer my thoughts about the Christian life.

There is one unique aspect to the approach I intend to use that is the motivation for all I will share within these pages. I have a great desire to offer a highly *practical* as well as a fully *biblical* look at the Christian life. There are a couple of reasons why this is very important to me.

First, I have come to understand that the Christian life is an utterly practical endeavor in which we experience the reality of the living Jesus in our lives daily. Simply put, Christianity is Christ and the Christian life is all about knowing Him. For this reason, everything I share comes from a strong desire to encourage and impart a practical encounter with Jesus that leads to a transformed life. We need to know the Lord in truth and then apply our faith toward Him in a deeply devotional and intimate way. I hope that as you read and interact with the truth in this book it will be as though you are "beholding as in a mirror the glory of the Lord, and are being transformed into the same image from glory to glory" (2 Cor. 3:18).

Second, I want to present a fully biblical approach to everything I share. Ever since I met Jesus in 1986, I have always had a very great desire to know the Scriptures. This led me in the direction of studying which culminated in a PhD in Evangelism and New Testament in 1997. Most of my studying companions went on to pursue posts in academic settings such as lecturers, researchers, and administrators, while the Lord led me into the mission field. After many years of practical ministry in various settings, including mission training schools, local churches, and leadership conferences in rural areas in all of the countries in eastern and southern Africa as well as countries in Europe, Asia, and South America, I have come to believe that there is a dire need throughout the body of Christ for believers to be more firmly grounded in the truth of the Scriptures.

Each and every one of us has a unique journey with the Lord. As time passes, He directs our lives and leads us on a personal path. This does not make any one of us better or worse than the other. It is a simple fact that we are all different. I acknowledge that my journey with the Lord has been one that first led me through a season of rigorous academic studies. I was fortunate to come through those years not only with my faith intact but also with a passion to know Jesus more. As a result of my experiences, I offer a unique lens through which to view the Christian life. It is one that combines a profound personal encounter with Jesus and a deep understanding of the Scriptures. I hope this perspective encourages you and empowers you to see things in a new and life-giving way.

This book contains a lot of Scripture! I am always reminded of what Jesus said to the Pharisees about the Scriptures:

> "You search the Scriptures because you think
> that in them you have eternal life; it is these that
> testify about Me; and you are unwilling to come
> to Me so that you may have life" (John 5:39-40).

In our efforts to understand and learn more about God through His word, we need to be careful to not be like the Pharisees. We should always remember that it is Jesus who ultimately gives us revelation by His Spirit so that we can know Him better. The most important thing is to come to Him. As we do this, the Scriptures do what they are meant to do—reveal more of Jesus.

I desire to help you see how the Scriptures testify directly to the reality of the life of Jesus that is already within you as a believer. Our interaction with the Scriptures is never an end in itself. As we unearth the truth in the Scriptures, they will propel us further into our practical encounter with Him.

I would also say from the very outset that this is not a complete expression of everything I believe concerning our life as believers. Sharing all the areas of the Christian life lies far outside the work of one book. There are many things that I will not discuss in these pages. These include things like healthy emotional development, spiritual disciplines (like prayer, Scripture meditation, and contemplation), and the practical functioning of each member in the body of Christ, just to name a few. These and other important topics will have to wait for some future discussion as the Lord may lead.

The Scripture references throughout the book are obviously there to offer biblical support for everything I share. They are also there for your benefit. I encourage you to take the time to read these Scriptures as you make your way through each chapter.

This book will not, like many others, progress as a story or a development of a specific theme. It is, on the other hand, a presentation of the truth as it relates to several of the most important aspects of our spiritual identity. I also do not present these in a suggested order of importance. They may seem at first to be unrelated or disconnected from one another. But they are actually intricately connected, and together they serve as the building blocks of our identity as children of God.

Here are some of the questions I will address. These are questions that I hear over and over again as I spend time with Christians in many different places around the world.

- Does God have a purpose for my life?

- What does it mean to live by faith?

- How do I receive the grace of God in my life?

- What is the role of the Holy Spirit in my life?

- What does it mean to be righteous?

- How many of my sins have been forgiven, and how do I experience God's forgiveness?

- Do I have to confess my sins to God in order for Him to forgive me?

- How do I live free from sin?

- Why do I still struggle with sin in my life after becoming a Christian?

- Why is life so hard, even when you are a Christian?

- Is there a way to experience true peace and rest in my life?

If I accomplish anything with this book, I want to bring you closer to Jesus Christ. Since He is the very foundation of life (1 Cor. 3:11) and all truth proceeds from and through Him (John 14:6), it is only fitting that everything focuses on Him. I believe that as you read through each chapter you will have a very real sense of God building something substantial into your life.

As I have already said, I want to connect you to the Word of God and the Holy Spirit who will lead you into all the truth (John 16:13). I don't want this to come across as only an academic study, nor simply a devotional book. I want it to facilitate a process in which you will encounter the power of the truth of the Word as it is applied to your heart by the activity of the Holy Spirit and the life of Christ within you!

Each chapter will end with a short devotional section. *Encountering the Truth* will help you to renew your mind by engaging a key truth from the chapter as well as offer a faith declaration that you can use to establish this truth in your life. *Walking in the Truth* will give you practical steps in how to walk in the truth of each chapter on a daily basis.

My prayer is that you will be encouraged and strengthened, and that you will find yourself more in love with Jesus and freshly amazed by His unfathomable riches (Eph. 3:8). Thank you for taking the time to read. I believe it will be worth it.

INTRODUCTION

Jesus said, "I am the way, the truth, and the life" (John 14:6); and "when He, the Spirit of truth, comes, He will guide you into all the truth" (John 16:13); and "you will know the truth, and the truth will make you free" (John 8:32). Having a true knowledge of Jesus brings a wealth that comes from the full assurance of understanding because all the treasures of wisdom and understanding are hidden in Him (Col. 2:2)!

I can clearly remember my experience of becoming a Christian and starting a personal relationship with God. It was in June 1986 when I prayed and acknowledged my own personal need for Jesus. At that time, thirty-four years ago, I obviously had very little understanding or revelation into what being a Christian was really all about. Like many people, I thought it was mostly about getting my life fixed so that things would go better for me in the future. And at that point in my life I really needed that! In addition to getting my life sorted out, I would also get eternity with God, commonly referred to as my "ticket to heaven." It all made perfect sense at the time, and my response to give my life to the Lord was significant and genuine.

I set out to begin living my newfound life with the Lord. I quickly learned from many well-meaning people what they believed were necessary activities and disciplines for a Christian. These included reading my Bible regularly, praying daily, giving my time and money in practical ways (including tithing), being an active member of a church, sharing my faith regularly, and the list goes on and on. So, I became busy doing all those things. It was like I had a new job and over time I actually became pretty good at it.

It didn't take too long for me to recognize that doing all the right things didn't connect me to the life and reality of Jesus. As time went on, I also began to realize many ideas I had about God and the Christian life were incomplete, and some were just downright wrong. The last thirty-four years have been a continual journey of learning, growing, changing, and most of all, getting to know Jesus more.

Over all these years, I have come to see a little more clearly. I have encountered the truth and it has set me free. I have also learned that while all truth is in Jesus, the truth contains many deep and profound truths that should shape our beliefs and understanding about God and who we are as believers. Without the truth well established in our lives, we struggle to experience life as God intends for us to experience it.

There are a multitude of topics that relate to the Christian life. Many of them are important and profitable, although not all of them are essential. I don't presume that the topics that I will discuss here are an exhaustive list or that they contain all truth. These are the truths that I have found to be extremely important as I have sought to know God more and to experience the gift of life He has given me in Jesus Christ. They are *Essential Truth.*

To say something is essential means that it is absolutely necessary or of extreme importance. To say something is essential also implies some things are non-essential. How do

I distinguish the difference? I would say that anything in our relationship with God that we can produce out of our own effort is a non-essential. This means that the topics in this book are things that God has accomplished through His own doing for our benefit. It is the truth that rises out of the life and finished work of Jesus Christ on behalf of all mankind. To say it is essential means that it is vital to us enjoying the life that God originally intended for us. This is probably the most important thing for you to keep in mind as you read this book.

Essential truth is critical to us experiencing the Christian life in a way that brings transformation and deep meaning. It is not a list of things you do, but it is the truth you encounter, believe, and allow to shape your life.

In what we call the Sermon on the Mount, Jesus declared that a man's house is only as secure as the foundation on which it is built (Matt. 7:24-27). The Apostle Paul said, "...no man can lay a foundation other than the one which is laid, which is Jesus Christ" (1 Cor. 3:11). I want to stay as close to this foundation as possible and build with gold, silver, and precious stones so that my work will remain (1 Cor. 3:14).

This is not a "how to" book about Christian living. The last thing I want to do is to leave you with the impression or burden that there is more for you to do in order to be a better Christian. Rather, I want to share with you powerful and life-giving truth that, by believing, your life can be transformed into His likeness (Rom. 8:29), and you will be able to run with endurance the race set before you (Heb. 12:1).

Jesus also said that we will know the truth and the truth will make us free (John 8:32). The word "know" jumps out at me when I read this verse. I have come to understand it is by *knowing the truth* that the truth makes us free. My desire is to help you encounter the truth. Your responsibility is to know and to believe the truth so it can make you free.

My spiritual journey has given me a deeply meaningful and personal relationship with Jesus Christ. I have also experienced life-changing and lasting transformation as a result of beholding His glory (2 Cor. 3:18). This transformation is based on many revelations of the truth that I know are both lasting and transformative because they are not tied to something I do or don't do. They are directly related to who Jesus is and what He has done.

This is what I call the process of "spiritual formation." Spiritual formation must happen if you are ever going to experience life in Christ as God intends it and grow into "the measure of the stature which belongs to the fullness of Christ" (Eph. 4:13). Spiritual formation does not take place through religious activities like going to church, reading your Bible, and living a good life. Spiritual formation only happens as we come to the Lord in complete faith and encounter the living Jesus on a daily basis.

Prepare your own heart for the truth you are about to encounter. It might be new, different, or challenging compared to what you have heard so far in your Christian journey. If you will open your mind and ask the Spirit to teach you as you progress through this book, I believe it will be a huge blessing to you. Let's go on this journey together and see where it takes us.

1

PURPOSE

As we discover what it means to live in His eternal outlook, and view the parts as they are related to the whole, we shall see how imperative it is to have the proper starting point.

                                    ~ DeVern Fromke

This was in accordance with the eternal purpose which He carried out in Christ Jesus our Lord, in whom we have boldness and confident access through faith in Him.

                                    ~ Ephesians 3:11-12

Have you ever asked the question, "What is my purpose in life?" This question lies deep in the heart of every person. The Westminster Confession of 1647 asks this question, "What is the chief end of man?" It then answers with, "Man's chief end is to glorify God, and to enjoy him forever."

People are hungry for an answer to this age-old question. Rick Warren's 2002 book, *The Purpose Driven Life: What on Earth Am I Here For?*, confirms this. It very simply presented what Warren says are God's five purposes for human life on earth—and it sold over 18 million copies!

There is no doubt that God has purpose in everything He does. We see this throughout the Bible. Job said of God, "I know that You can do all things, and that no purpose of Yours can be thwarted" (Job 42:2). In the garden of Gethsemane, Jesus asked the Father to save Him from His time of suffering, but He ultimately said, "...for this purpose I came to this hour" (John 12:27). Peter and John said in Acts 4 that many were gathered in Jerusalem to do harm to Jesus, including "Herod and Pontius Pilate, along with the Gentiles and the peoples of Israel, to do whatever Your hand and Your purpose predestined to occur" (Acts 4:27-28). Paul said he "did not shrink from declaring to you the whole purpose of God" (Acts 20:27). John told us, "The Son of God appeared for this purpose, to destroy the works of the devil" (1 John 3:8b). All of these verses illustrate that God acts according to what He purposes to do.

Purpose simply means that there is a reason why something is done. It should not come as a surprise to us that God acts according to what He purposes. He is not haphazard in the way that He goes about doing things. Because He has a reason for all that He does, we can say God has purpose in everything. This is evident from the very beginning when He created the first man and woman. We know that He said to Adam and Eve to "be fruitful and multiply, and fill the earth, and subdue it; and rule over the fish of the sea and over the birds of the sky and over every living thing that moves on the

earth" (Gen. 1:28). On one level we can say that this was part
of God's purpose for Adam and Eve. But there is something
else to notice about this story that is very important as it
relates directly to God's purpose for Adam and Eve.

Genesis 2:9 says,

> Out of the ground the Lord God caused to grow
> every tree that is pleasing to the sight and good
> for food; the tree of life also in the midst of the
> garden, and the tree of the knowledge of good
> and evil.

Then God commanded Adam saying,

> From any tree of the garden you may eat freely;
> but from the tree of the knowledge of good and
> evil you shall not eat, for in the day that you eat
> from it you will surely die. (Gen. 2:16-17).

Notice that Adam was completely free to eat from any tree
in the garden except one. This means that he was free to eat
from every other tree in the garden—and that included the
tree of life! In fact, God put it in the middle of the garden so
Adam would not miss it. His reason for putting the tree of life
in a place where Adam could easily find it reveals something
about God's purpose for Adam.

The first man and woman are representative of all
mankind. When Adam and Eve ate from the wrong tree,
God put them out of the garden and placed a cherubim and
a flaming sword to guard the way to the tree of life (Gen.
3:24). The fact that God would station an angel to guard this
tree shows us that it was very important in God's plan and
purpose. When they ate from the tree of the knowledge of

good and evil, God put Adam and Eve out of the garden until mankind would have another opportunity to eat from the tree of life. This happened when Jesus appeared bringing life to all men (John 1:4; John 10:10; Rom. 5:18).

The ultimate purpose of God could not be revealed until, when "the fullness of time came, God sent forth His Son" (Gal. 4:4). Until that time, God's purpose was held in a mystery. Paul received a revelation of the mystery (Eph. 3:3), which he called "the mystery of Christ" (Eph. 3:4). According to Paul, this mystery was not made known to men in previous generations, but has now been revealed by the Spirit. One aspect of this mystery was that the Gentiles would be part of the body of Christ (Eph. 3:6). But this is not the central focus of the mystery. Paul went on to say that he was called to preach "the unfathomable riches of Christ, and to bring to light what is the administration of the mystery which for ages has been hidden in God" (Eph. 3:8-9).

God hid the mystery for generations "so that the manifold wisdom of God might now be made known through the church to the rulers and authorities in the heavenly places" (Eph. 3:10). All this was done in "accordance with the eternal purpose which He carried out in Christ Jesus our Lord" (Eph. 3:11). This phrase, "eternal purpose," literally means "the purpose of the ages." This is the purpose of all purposes!

Let's begin to tie this all together. Paul said,

> ...the mystery which has been hidden from the past ages and generations, but has now been manifested to His saints, to whom God willed to make known what is the riches of the glory of

this mystery among the Gentiles, which is Christ
in you, the hope of glory (Col. 1:26-27).

Do you see it? The unveiling of the mystery, which is in
accordance with the purpose of the ages, is *Christ in you, the
hope of glory.*

Jesus said that He came that we may have life, and have
it abundantly (John 10:10). One of the most famous Bible
verses says, "... that whoever believes in Him shall not perish,
but have eternal life" (John 3:16). Eternal life does not only
refer to the quantity (or length) of life. It is the quality of life
that Jesus gives. It is the life of God that never dies. What
God desired from the very beginning through the tree of
life in the garden of Eden is now made possible through the
Lord Jesus Christ. The purpose of the ages is that we would
share in the life of God with Him.

Remember the question at the beginning of this chapter,
"What is my purpose in life?" Now we will begin to bring the
answer to this question into focus. Paul said,

> Blessed be the God and Father of our Lord Jesus
> Christ, who has blessed us with every spiritual
> blessing in the heavenly places in Christ, just
> as He chose us in Him before the foundation of
> the world, that we would be holy and blameless
> before Him (Eph. 1:3-4).

Notice three things in these verses. First, God "chose us."
Second, He chose us "in Him" (Jesus). Third, He chose us in
Him "before the foundation of the world." This means that
God decided *before* He ever created anything to choose us
in Christ. This is an amazing thought and a powerful truth.

But Paul did not stop there. He went on to say that "He predestined us to adoption as sons through Jesus Christ to Himself, according to the kind intention of His will" (Eph. 1:5). We shouldn't get hung up on this word "predestined." Debates have raged throughout church history over what it means. (The last thing I want to do is to get caught up in that debate.) The word means "to determine something before." God still gives us freedom to choose and will not violate our ability to do so. This is the foundation of relationship. There must always be choice. But the fact remains, before God made anything, He first decided to choose us in Christ! This is a beautiful truth.

Paul goes on in this passage to say that God chose us to become sons and daughters because of His kindness and for the glory of His grace. He concluded these first verses of Ephesians 1 by saying that God chose us "according to His purpose" (Eph. 1:11).

What exactly does it mean to be chosen according to purpose? Most importantly, it means that we have a reason for living and that reason comes from God. God made sure that we have a purpose before the world was ever created. Now let's make the final connection and see what God's ultimate purpose is for our lives.

Romans 8:28 is commonly quoted by Christians in times when they need assurance that God can bring good out of difficult situations. This verse says, "And we know that God causes all things to work together for good to those who love God, to those who are called *according to His purpose*." It is a magnificent promise that God causes all things to work together for good. But notice how the verse ends. It happens for those who love God, to those who are called "according to His purpose." There it is again. We are called according to His purpose.

This is where many of us make one of the most common mistakes in reading the Bible. We stop in the middle of a thought. We like what we hear and we just camp out there. But keep reading. The next verse says,

> For those whom He foreknew, He also predestined to become conformed to the image of His Son, so that He would be the firstborn among many brethren (Rom. 8:29).

There is that word "predestined" again. It is the same word we saw in Ephesians 1. And now Paul is telling us that God also decided beforehand that we would be conformed to the image of His Son.

Before the world was ever created, God chose us in Christ. He did this because He had a purpose to accomplish. His purpose was that we would share in His life. It is what He wanted from the very beginning when He put the tree of life in the middle of the garden. He not only wants us to partake of His life, but He wants us to be like Him. God's desire is that we know and express His life as His sons and daughters, and He uses everything that happens in our lives to accomplish this purpose. Let me illustrate the application of Romans 8:28:

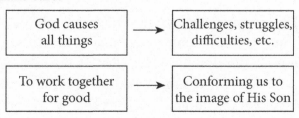

When we look at it this way, the "good" that happens is God conforming us to the image of Jesus. It does not mean everything works out for us in a good and happy way and we get what we want. It means the ultimate good that comes is we are becoming more like Jesus! This makes the promise of Romans 8:28-29 more meaningful than ever.

God has no higher purpose than for His Son to be glorified in and through all things, especially our lives! He desires nothing more than for His children to be like His only Son so that He can have a beautiful family of sons and daughters. God is passionate about His purpose and He will not stop this work in our lives until we all have His likeness and are expressing His life.

When this purpose grips your heart, you will never live the same again. This is not a theological ideal. It is the most practical explanation of God's deepest desire and ultimate purpose for mankind. It is the one single purpose that motivates everything the Father does. He *will* see His Son glorified in and through all things (Col. 1:16, 18). And the most exciting thing about it is that you get to participate in it all. In fact, "the anxious longing of the creation waits eagerly for the revealing of the sons of God" (Rom. 8:19). This means that everything that has been created by God is sitting on pins and needles waiting for you to become a mature son or daughter who expresses the life of Christ.

We can miss the real meaning of God's purpose for our lives if we only understand it in terms of (1) our salvation; (2) our destiny; or (3) what we do. Salvation is not God's ultimate purpose for mankind. It doesn't make sense to say that God's end goal for us is that we be saved. This assumes that when God created man and woman He created them to be saved. But Adam and Eve originally had no need of salvation when they were created—salvation cannot be God's ultimate purpose for creating mankind. It is surely part of the process of God bringing us to the point where we can participate in His initial plan, but it is not His original and ultimate intention. Salvation is certainly necessary as a corrective measure to deal with the devastating effects of sin in the world. But we should not think of it as the greatest purpose of God for our lives because God has an even bigger plan. This plan centers in Jesus filling all things.

Purpose is also not the same as destiny. Since I became a Christian, I have often heard people talk about destiny. They focus on the need to pursue their destiny so that they can realize all God has for them. They become preoccupied with the notion that God has a specific, unique path for their lives and that all their experiences are meant to bring them into their destiny. I am not totally sure, but it seems to me that people are talking about an ideal of what their life is going to look like at some point in the future. When they arrive there, they will experience their God-given destiny.

"Destiny" has to do with the hidden power believed to control what will happen in the future (i.e., fate). The Bible actually has very little to say about destiny. A quick search reveals that the word "destiny" only appears in one verse. Isaiah 65:11-12 says,

> "But you who forsake the Lord, who forget My holy mountain, who set a table for Fortune, and who fill cups with mixed wine for Destiny, I will destine you for the sword, and all of you will bow down to the slaughter."

This one reference to "destiny" in the Bible speaks directly to those who have forsaken the Lord by refusing to seek Him. Instead, they have turned to their own table of Fortune and drink from the cup of Destiny. This doesn't sound very positive.

The word "Destiny" in this verse in Isaiah is the Hebrew word *Meni* and it actually refers to an ancient pagan god. Meni was a god of good luck—possibly the Pleiades— found in ancient astrology. It is believed that the ancients worshipped the constellations in hope of securing some good fortune for their future. Thus, their destiny was wrapped up in the stars! It is the same idea that many people today refer to as their zodiac sign. God does not want us looking to the stars to find our purpose.

Finally, many people are under the impression that their purpose is what they do. I think this is a mindset that most of us can relate to. When I was younger, I wanted to know what it was that I would eventually be doing in life. Because I could not answer that question in my early 20s, I struggled to have direction and often wondered what my purpose was. We might say of someone like that, "They don't have any purpose." We don't mean that they would be better off dead. We mean they haven't found that "something" to do that will give them meaning and motivation. In doing this, we confuse purpose with a vocation or career.

On the surface this sounds fine and good. But what happens when we change careers, which most people do several times throughout their lifetime? Does our purpose change? Or even worse, what if something happens and we are unable to continue doing our job? Have we lost our meaning in life? If we understand purpose as something that we do, we will struggle to find the ultimate fulfillment God wants us to find. He knows the reason why we were made. He created us to become like His Son. Becoming more like Jesus is the only thing that will bring fulfillment and give us a deep sense of well-being in our hearts and minds. This is God's design for us and the only thing that gives us purpose for being.

The great thing about the purpose of God is that He is working it in your life all the time (Phil. 2:13). You do not have to wait for certain events to happen for you to have purpose. The purpose of God is not a unique calling or vocation. It is not a specific outcome where you experience your destiny and all of a sudden life takes on special meaning because of your circumstances.

None of these could be further from the truth about God's purpose. He is working it in your life through all your circumstances, the good and the difficult. You have the privilege and opportunity to align yourself with His purpose each and every day.

The purpose of God is for you to experience His life and to become more like Jesus every day.

The beauty about the purpose of God is that it never changes. It is not something you have to struggle to understand. It is simple—yet profound. His goal is that you know Him more and that as He lives through you, you experience His transforming power in your life every day.

Once you get this settled in your mind and heart, it changes everything. Now your attention is on how God is working in and through all the circumstances in your life to accomplish His purpose for you to be like Jesus. I tell people all the time, when you finally get this revelation and start living life according to God's purpose, there is only one question that really matters. I ask myself this question almost daily, "What does God want to do in my life through this circumstance to help me become more like Jesus?"

When you ask this question, you shift your focus away from your circumstances or what you are doing in life and begin to align yourself with God's objective. I can testify that this is challenging to do. It is not easy because God is going to expose areas of your life that are not like Jesus!

I can remember a time when Stephanie and I were having some real difficulties in our relationship. I was at a very low point and was crying out to God. I was asking Him why we were struggling so much in our marriage. (Notice I was asking the wrong question. But God is patient and kind, and He will help lead us to the right place.) I believe I heard God speak to me more clearly than I have ever heard Him before or since. He asked me this question; "Cliff, do you want to know why you are continuing to struggle in your marriage?" I said, "Yes!" He then said, "The problem is that *you are not like Me.*"

That was my undoing! I had been a Christian for over twenty years. I was in full-time ministry and had taught many people about the things of the Lord. I had spent many years growing and maturing in my relationship with God. And now the Lord was telling me I was not like Him. That was the day when God started teaching me what I am sharing with you in this chapter. He showed me that Jesus is a perfect husband to my wife and that the more I was conformed to

His image, He would be Stephanie's husband through me! I received the revelation, humbled myself, repented, and started allowing Jesus to love Stephanie through me. That is where this journey began for me and that is where God began to restore our marriage.

Your purpose in life is to encounter Jesus in a life-transforming way. You are called to participate personally in the life of God so that you can experience the design of God to make you more like Jesus. Only God can change your heart, motives, attitudes, and behaviors. This is the promise of the gospel. You have been called according to His purpose and this purpose is your greatest reason for living.

I believe this is the longing deep in the heart of every person because it is the reason why we were created. We all want to know that we can really be transformed and find fulfillment. This is only found in Jesus. He is the life-transforming power of God living within you to conform you into His very likeness. This is God's purpose for you and it is an essential truth of the Christian life.

Encountering the Truth

Truth: Everything God does in your life is according to His eternal purpose which He determined before the foundation of the world. This purpose of the ages is that you would experience His life through Jesus and be more like Him.

Faith Declaration: I am called according to God's purpose, and He is using every situation in my life to conform me to the image of Christ.

🚶 *Walking in the Truth*

Begin to set your mind on the truth that God has a wonderful purpose for you. Each day recognize that God is using every situation, circumstance, challenge, and relationship to work His purpose deep into your life. He will use every opportunity to make you more like Jesus. Begin to ask the Lord, "How do you want to use what I am going through right now to make me more like Jesus?" Ask the Lord to give you wisdom, understanding, and self-awareness of those areas in your life that He is busy with each day. Agree with the truth that His life is in you, transforming you, and that you want to know and express His life to others for His glory.

2

PERSPECTIVE

"You take the blue pill, the story ends. You wake up in your bed and believe whatever you want to believe. You take the red pill, you stay in Wonderland, and I show you how deep the rabbit hole goes."

~ *Morpheus* - The Matrix

The Matrix Trilogy was one of the most popular movie series in the last twenty years. In case you did not see any of the movies, I will explain the basic story line. The writers of the movies suggest that through man's ultimate advancement he created a world in which machines ruled. What man did not expect was that the machines would take over the world. This hostile takeover marks the end of the physical world as we know it. It is reduced to a dark and deserted war zone. In their attempt to live on, the machines create a parallel universe based inside the virtual reality of a computer. Humans are then cultivated in water pods and their energy is harvested as the power source that drives the computer, which in turn communicates this virtual reality into the minds of the humans who are simply lying lifelessly in water-filled energy pods. Morpheus and his team rescue people from the computer-generated virtual world—the Matrix—by giving them a red pill that extracts them from their energy pod and releases them back into what remains of the real human world. In this place, the rescued people live together in a community called Zion. If people choose to take the blue pill, they stay in their water-filled energy pod, remain in the Matrix, and never know the difference. The movies aren't Christian, but they do contain many spiritual analogies. The most obvious to me is how people in the Matrix are bound by what the computer world tells them, but with a shift in perspective (taking the red pill) everything changes.

Being a Christian is so much more than having your sins forgiven and receiving a "ticket to heaven" someday when you die. As good as this is, it really doesn't do justice to all that God has done for you through Jesus Christ.

The truth is that when you become a Christian you undergo a huge shift in your actual existence. You have taken the red pill and it is time for you to see how deep the rabbit hole goes. As you travel down the rabbit hole—metaphorically speaking—and discover what it means to be a Christian, you find out how important it is to see things from God's perspective. Before you believed in Jesus, "the god of this world had blinded the minds of the unbelieving" (2 Cor. 4:4) from seeing properly. But now through the gracious work of God's Spirit, you are able to see. This ability to see brings a completely new perspective. God does not want us to remain in our old way of perceiving things. There is so much more that He wants us to see, and it is possible as we understand what He has done within us to give us His perspective.

As long as I can remember I have loved flying in planes. Being so high in the air and looking down gives you such a different perspective on things. I always imagine what it must be like to see things the way God sees them. Having God's vantage point is super important. Unfortunately, it is something that many of us fail to consider on a daily basis. When you look at things differently and see them from the eternal perspective of spiritual truth, it makes a huge difference in your life.

In His well-known conversation with Nicodemus in John 3, Jesus said, "Truly, truly, I say to you, unless one is born again he cannot see the kingdom of God" (John 3:3). For over two thousand years of Christian history, the idea of being "born again" is probably the most common way to refer to what happens when someone believes in Jesus. Unfortunately, a lot of Christians do not fully understand the depth of what it means to be born again. The main reason for this is that—like so much of the truth about the Christian life—being born again speaks to a spiritual reality that cannot be understood with your natural mind. But just because you cannot know it through your natural senses does not make it any less real. In fact, the spiritual truth of being born again is just as real as anything you encounter in the natural realm.

The very phrase "born again" implies that there is actually a new life that did not exist prior to becoming a Christian. You don't have to feel bad if you do not understand exactly what this means—traveling down the rabbit hole can sometimes be a confusing adventure. Even Nicodemus struggled to understand what Jesus was saying. He responded to Jesus in the same way that some of us feel like responding, how can you possibly enter again into your mother's womb?! The fact that Nicodemus asked this question proves that he was not thinking spiritually, but in an earthly, natural way.

Jesus wants you to see things as He sees them and not as you see them with your natural senses. For this to happen there has to be a new birth. The new birth by the Spirit gives you the ability to see the kingdom of God. This opens up an entire new way of perceiving everything that happens in your life.

The reality is that God has caused a spiritual birth to take place within you. This means that you literally have a life in the Spirit that is brand new and whose source is God Himself. Jesus said, "That which is born of the flesh is flesh, and that which is born of the Spirit is spirit" (John 3:6), and John said that those who believe in His name are "born, not of blood nor of the will of the flesh nor of the will of man, but of God" (John 1:13).

The implications of this are huge. You are now made alive by the Spirit, and your spirit has been joined inseparably to the Lord (1 Cor. 6:17). You have a new spiritual existence, and you must learn to shift your point of view to this new life within if you are going to live in the fullness that God wants for you. If you don't allow this shift of perspective in your life, you will stay stuck in the Matrix, the natural thinking of the world, and you will miss much of what God wants you to see and experience.

In 2 Corinthians 5:17 Paul tells us, "Therefore if anyone is in Christ, he is a new creature; the old things passed away; behold, new things have come." This verse also speaks about the new birth. The new birth expresses itself in the reality of a new creation.

The "new man" is Paul's favorite way to refer to this reality in the life of the believer. If we are not careful, we can fall into the trap of thinking that Paul is a male chauvinist talking only about the "new man" and not the "new woman" as well. And believe me, many have jumped on that bandwagon and caused a lot of damage within the body of Christ.

In the original language of the New Testament, there are two words that are translated "man." The first is the Greek word *anér*. This word means a "male human being" or a "man." The second is the Greek word *anthrópos*. This word means a "human being" or "human mankind" in a general sense, including man and woman. *Anthrópos* is the word that Paul used when he spoke about the "new man" (Eph. 4:24; Rom. 6:6; Col. 3:9). By using this word, Paul was saying that we are actually part of a completely new human race! This is a wonderful truth and one that calls for a huge shift in our thinking. It is also a truth that has nothing to do with male and female (Gal. 3:28). When he talked about the "new man," Paul was not referring to men only, but to all who are a part of this new race in Christ, male and female.

When you become a Christian, you instantly become part of this new race in Jesus. It is not something that you try to obtain after becoming a Christian. It is something that

God does in you and it happens through faith. Once you have made this shift in your belief, you then discover how it impacts your life in practical ways.

Paul said,

> ...in reference to your former manner of life, you lay aside the old self (*anthrópos*), which is being corrupted in accordance with the lusts of deceit, and that you be renewed in the spirit of your mind, and put on the new self (*anthrópos*), which in the likeness of God has been created in righteousness and holiness of the truth (Eph. 4:22-24).

This is one of my favorite verses about the new man. I have used this verse as a powerful tool in my own life to help me enter into this life-changing truth. Paul used a simple metaphor in these verses of dressing and undressing. It is something so practical that all of us can understand because we do it every day in the natural. We take clothes off and we put clothes on. To help us connect to this spiritual truth, Paul was saying that in a practical/spiritual way we need to take off the old man and put on the new man. The new man is already a reality. This is why Paul said the new man "*has been created* in righteousness and holiness of the truth" (Eph. 4:24). We simply exercise our faith every day and put him on. I do this in my own devotional times with the Lord. I envision myself taking off the old man and putting on the new man. It is critical that we do something practical each day that helps us to connect with this truth.

Once you truly believe that you are literally a new human, you will begin to make the practical shift in your daily living.

Simply put, you must believe that you are a new person and regularly apply your faith towards this essential truth. As you apply your faith and believe the truth, your knowledge of the truth will increase within you, and your personal interaction with the truth will begin to set you free.

This is how the Lord works in your life to bring about transformation. He leads you to the truth and then asks you to believe it. In response to the expression of your faith in the truth, God begins to do the very thing in your life that you are believing. The actualization of the truth increases in direct proportion to your faith in it! When you grasp the power of your faith in this way, it will transform the way you live.

In this process you need to keep in mind that your faith is never greater than the truth. The truth has the power to set you free and your faith is the key to access this power. The true gospel of the New Testament must have at its core this understanding of faith. Faith is the centerpiece of your Christian experience and without it you will never have a personal encounter with the truth that manifests in your life and brings about transformation.

Once you begin to understand who you really are as a new creation, you will adjust your thinking and start seeing things differently. It's as if you put on the right pair of glasses and everything suddenly becomes clear.

The shift we have experienced in our inner being will impact our daily lives on a very practical level. The main way this happens is when we start looking at our circumstances differently. We all have an innate propensity to look with our eyes, both physically and symbolically, at what is going on around us. If we don't shift our perspective, we will never make significant steps in our spiritual growth. I touched on this in the previous chapter when I explained how God uses our circumstances to make us more like Jesus.

Paul said,

> ...we look not at the things which are seen, but at the things which are not seen; for the things which are seen are temporal, but the things which are not seen are eternal (2 Cor. 4:18).

This is one of those verses that may seem quite strange at first. You might ask, "How can I stop looking at things that are seen and start looking at things that are not seen?" This is a normal question to ask and there is a good answer.

The answer is that you have to learn how to live according to your new nature as a spiritual person. You have to make a fundamental—and sometimes really hard—choice to stop looking at things only as you see them in the natural realm. Your natural vision is an effective and necessary sense. However, it was never intended to be used as the means by which you see and perceive things from God's perspective.

In addition to your eyes, you also use your reason and emotions to assess your circumstances. But God does not want you to use your physical vision, your reason, or your emotions to look at things. On the contrary, God has opened the eyes of your heart (Acts 26:18; 2 Cor. 4:6; Eph. 1:18), and you are now able to see in a totally different way. You are actually able to see and to perceive things from an eternal perspective. This does not mean you ignore what you see and feel. It just means you learn that there is a better way.

There is a truth here that you cannot afford to miss. The truth is that the things which you can see with your natural eyes are only temporal, and the things you see with your spiritual eyes are eternal. This has profound implications for you as a believer. As long as you are busy looking at things with your natural eyes, you are only looking at earthly things which are destined to pass away. Temporal perspective never gives you the whole story. You need to learn to look with your spiritual eyes so you can see eternal things. Eternal things contain truth and keep you living from God's perspective.

Let's consider this truth in a very practical way. Your circumstances at any point in time are real. You are not called to ignore them and act like they do not exist. God does not want you to walk in denial. However, if you only look at the circumstances around you, create your judgments, and make your decisions based on what you see in the natural, you can be assured that those circumstances will always change and your judgments will be based on limited, partial knowledge at best. This is why you need to develop a healthy and mature approach to what you see going on around you.

As you develop the ability to look at things that are unseen, your perspective begins to change. Things that are unseen are those things that pertain to God and His eternal perspective. We know that God's perspective is totally complete because He sees all things from the beginning until the end.

Paul also told us,

> Therefore if you have been raised up with Christ, keep seeking the things above, where Christ is, seated at the right hand of God. Set your mind on the things above, not on the things that are on earth (Col. 3:1-2).

This is another encouragement for us to shift our perspective. You can actually choose where to set your mind. When you make that choice and shift your focus to things above, you will realize that your life is actually there with Christ where He is seated!

This became a deep-rooted truth for my wife and me through the life of our special-needs son, Wesley. Some who will read this book know Wesley personally. He is a beautiful young man and brings life and joy wherever he is. But Wesley has a genetic disorder called Fragile X that extremely limits his cognitive ability. In this life, apart from a miracle, he will never be able to read, write, and reason like other full functioning people. Early in his life God showed us the truth about Wesley to encourage us as his parents. The truth is that God loves Wesley as he is and what we see in Wesley's life is only temporary. It is a condition that is true in this life only. Wesley will be complete, without disability, forever in eternity. This shift in perspective brings so much peace and hope as we walk this journey with Wesley. Our perspective has shifted, and we experience the blessing of seeing Wesley—and his amazing value—as God sees him.

One of my favorite stories in the Old Testament that illustrates this truth tangibly is the story of Elisha and his attendant in 2 Kings 6. Elisha's attendant rose early in the morning and went out and saw an army of horses and chariots circling the city. Filled with fear, he came to Elisha to give him the news of what he had seen. Elisha had the greatest response:

> "Do not fear, for those who are with us are more than those who are with them." Then Elisha prayed and said, "O Lord, I pray, open his eyes that he may see." And the Lord opened

the servant's eyes and he saw; and behold, the
mountain was full of horses and chariots of fire
all around Elisha (2 Kings 6:16-17).

This is a perfect example of the difference between
looking with your natural eyes at things that are seen and
looking with your spiritual eyes at things that are not seen.
In the same way, God has opened your eyes so that you can
see things that are unseen. This allows you to take part in the
eternal things of God. You need to make the shift in your
perspective and start looking at things the way God wants
you to see them.

This does not mean that you will always have a
supernatural, tangible experience like Elisha's attendant. It
starts as you take little steps to shift your awareness and change
your focus. The Lord will help you to see your circumstances
differently. Over time you will become familiar with this
process and be able to discern the difference between seeing
things from God's spiritual, eternal perspective and your
natural, temporal perspective.

We have the mind of Christ (1 Cor. 2:16). Having the
mind of Christ empowers us to know all the things
that God has given us. These things are revealed to us by the
Spirit. Having the mind of Christ also means that we are able
to see and understand things the way God does. As we grow
and learn how to live in this truth, we begin to look at things
differently.

A sure mark of spiritual maturity is seeing with God's
perspective. Paul told the believers in Corinth that he could
not speak to them as "spiritual men" because they were
"men of flesh" in their thinking (1 Cor. 3:1-4). They were

judging between Peter, Paul, and Apollos, as to whom they preferred. This is a practical example of how we can look at things incorrectly because of wrong thinking. Paul set them straight by telling them that neither he, Peter, nor Apollos were anything, but Jesus was all that mattered. They were simply servants who helped them come to faith in Christ (1 Cor. 3:5). It took a spiritual man like Paul to help the believers in Corinth to stop looking at things in the natural and start seeing them from a spiritual perspective.

Having God's mindset in life is an essential part of your spiritual maturity. God fully understands that you are in this world and that it is an unavoidable reality that you interact with life on a very natural, physical level. However, He also wants you to know that there is a reality that exists now that is outside of this natural world. Being "born of the Spirit" (John 3:5-6) and being in Christ changes everything. It reorients you to a new perspective that permeates every area of your life.

🧠 Encountering the Truth

Truth: Your life has been completely changed as a result of your faith in Christ. You are a new creation and God wants your perspective in life to be shaped by the reality of who you are in Christ.

Faith Declaration: I am a new creation, I have the mind of Christ, and I am able to discern and understand things from God's perspective.

🚶 Walking in the Truth

At the start of every day, practice the faith step of putting on the new man. Make the decision today that you are not going to only focus on what is going on around you in the natural. Begin to believe that God is busy doing many things that you cannot see with your natural senses. By faith, ask God to give you His perspective. Believe that you have the mind of Christ and are able to understand things from God's viewpoint. Shift your perspective and let it impact the way you live each day.

3

GRACE

For of His fullness we have all received, and grace upon grace.

~ John 1:16

For if by the transgression of the one, death reigned through the one, much more those who receive the abundance of grace and of the gift of righteousness will reign in life through the One, Jesus Christ.

~ Romans 5:17

The giving of gifts is a common practice in most cultures around the world. Whether it is a birthday, anniversary, Christmas, or another special occasion, we give gifts to show our love and appreciation for others. Gifts can vary in value, but the most important thing about any gift is what the giver desires to communicate through the gift. Everyone loves receiving a gift that makes them feel greatly valued. God assigns the highest value for us through the gift He gives— the gift of life through His only Son.

Paul said,

> But the free gift is not like the transgression. For if by the transgression of the one the many died, much more did the *grace of God and the gift by the grace* of the one Man, Jesus Christ, abound to the many (Rom. 5:15).

The grace of God is the means by which God gives the greatest gift ever given. In this chapter you will discover the true meaning of grace and the profound impact it has on your life.

I know I have said it already, but it is worth saying again and again. God's highest desire is that you participate in His life with Him. The Father, Son, and Spirit want to share themselves fully and freely with you. Peter said that God has given you "precious and magnificent promises, so that by them you may become partakers of the divine nature" (2 Peter 1:4). God wants you to partake—to literally share—in His nature! This happens as you receive His life which He gives to you by grace.

You have probably seen this acronym:

G – God's
R – Riches (or Redemption)
A – At
C – Christ's
E – Expense

According to this definition of grace, Jesus paid a great price so that we can receive something very valuable from

God. For many of us this is pretty much the extent of our understanding of grace. It is true that Jesus paid a huge price for us to experience salvation. But there is much more to grace than this.

Before we jump into a discussion about grace in the life of a believer, I want to lay a biblical foundation for this essential truth. The most important thing to see is that grace specifically refers to the activity of God in and through Jesus Christ in the New Covenant. For this reason, from a biblical/ scriptural perspective, it is not appropriate for us to speak of grace in the context of the Old Testament. I am aware that this may sound strange at first, but I believe it is an important point to make as we seek to understand the true meaning of grace.

The Hebrew language and the culture of the Old Testament did not have a word or concept for grace. The closest word to grace in the Hebrew language is the word *chen* which means to "bestow favor upon or to show mercy to." Several different forms of this word appear almost 200 times in the Old Testament. Some examples of this word are when Lot found favor with the authorities in Sodom (Gen. 19:19); Jacob found favor with Esau (Gen. 32:5); Joseph found favor with Potiphar (Gen. 39:4); Ruth found favor with Boaz (Ruth 2:10); and David found favor with Jonathan (1 Sam. 20:3). In all these examples, people found favor with other people.

There are a few instances in the Old Testament where people found favor with God. For example, Noah (Gen. 6:8) and Moses (Ex. 33:12-13) are said to have found favor in God's sight. Gideon (Judges 6:17) and Samuel (1 Sam. 2:26) also found favor with the Lord. This is actually the most accurate way to translate the Hebrew word *chen*. Confusion about grace in the Old Testament comes in because some translations of the English Bible translate the Hebrew word *chen* as "grace." The translators simply decided to use "grace" instead of "favor" or "mercy" based on the context of the passage and their own understanding of grace. But this is not to say that God gave grace in the Old Testament.

God giving His grace to people is truly a New Testament and New Covenant phenomenon. This is why John started his gospel by telling us several key things about grace and how it relates to Jesus. He said that Jesus was full of "grace and truth" (John 1:14); that "of His fullness we have all received, grace upon grace" (John 1:16); and that "the Law was given through Moses; grace and truth were realized through Jesus Christ" (John 1:17). Paul confirmed this when he said, "…the grace of God has appeared, bringing salvation to all men" (Titus 2:11).

Grace became a reality when Jesus Christ appeared and it is only in Him that God gives His grace. Take a moment and read the following Scriptures carefully. I have added emphasis in these verses to highlight the truth about grace.

- For the Law was given through Moses; grace and truth were *realized through Jesus Christ* (John 1:17).

- "But we believe that we are saved *through the grace of the Lord Jesus*" (Acts 15:11).

- I thank my God always concerning you for *the grace* of God which was *given you in Christ Jesus* (1 Cor. 1:4).

- He predestined us to adoption as sons through Jesus Christ to Himself, according to the kind intention of

His will, to the praise of the glory of His *grace, which He freely bestowed on us in the Beloved* (Eph. 1:5-6).

- God who has saved us and called us with a holy call-ing, not according to our works, but according to His own purpose and *grace which was granted us in Christ Jesus* from all eternity (2 Tim. 1:9).

- The *grace of the Lord Jesus* be with all. Amen (Rev. 22:21).

Grace belongs to, comes from, and is given through Jesus Christ! It does us well to always keep in mind that Jesus Christ is the ultimate and final way that God relates to man (Heb. 1:1-2). When Jesus Christ came, everything changed. Seeing this difference is the key that unlocks our understanding of grace.

Now is a good time to make an observation about a difference between the Old Covenant and New Covenant. I will do this throughout the book because the difference between the Old and New Covenants affects the way we understand the Christian life. It is clear enough from the writers of the New Testament that there was a revolutionary shift in how man's relationship to God functions as a result of the New Covenant mediated by Jesus Christ (Heb. 8:6; 9:15; 12:24). (We will look in detail at what it means to be in a right relationship with God in Chapter 5 on Righteousness.) Paul said,

> ...nevertheless knowing that a man is not justified by the works of the Law but through faith in Christ Jesus, even we have believed in

Christ Jesus, so that we may be justified by faith
in Christ and not by the works of the Law; since
by the works of the Law no flesh will be justified
(Gal. 2:16).

The difference is clear. Under the Old Covenant "the
works of the Law" characterized man's relationship with
God. Under the New Covenant "faith in Christ Jesus"
characterizes our relationship with God. "Works" and "faith"
are counterparts in the two covenants (Rom. 3:27-28; Gal.
2:16; 3:2).

The main reason why God established the New Covenant
in Jesus Christ on the basis of faith is because He had already
made a promise to Abraham and to his seed based on
Abraham's faith. This is one of the most significant truths
about how God desires to relate to us. Paul said,

Now the promises were spoken to Abraham and
to his seed. He does not say, "And to seeds," as
referring to many, but rather to one, "And to
your seed," that is, Christ. What I am saying is
this: the Law, which came four hundred and
thirty years later, does not invalidate a covenant
previously ratified by God, so as to nullify the
promise (Gal. 3:16-17).

God had already made a promise to Abraham based
on his faith and that promise was also made to Jesus! The
promise was that whoever would have faith in Jesus, like
Abraham had faith in God, would be made righteous. This is
what it means to be justified. And this is why the Scriptures
teach that we are justified by faith in Christ Jesus and not by

the works of the law. The works of the law were never able to justify anyone (Rom. 3:20; Gal. 2:16; 3:11). This could only happen through faith in Christ (Rom. 3:26).

The important thing is that God's desire has always been for us to relate to Him by faith. The great faith chapter in Hebrews 11 clearly highlights this fact. From the very beginning it was faith that distinguished Abel's sacrifice from Cain's. And the writer of Hebrews rehearsed the many examples of faith in the lives of others in the Old Testament. The point is that God has never wanted us to relate to Him through our own efforts (i.e., works). He knows that everyone who attempts to do so will always fall short, so He justifies us "as a gift *by His grace* through the redemption which is in Christ Jesus" (Rom. 3:24). God does something for us that we could never do on our own—and that is grace! This is the foundation of the gospel and the greatest news anyone can ever hear. God has made perfect provision for us by His grace through Jesus Christ and all we have to do is believe it.

The life and finished work of Jesus Christ bring all of mankind back to the place of relating to God through faith. This is the work of grace. Faith is our response to what God has provided for us in Christ.

Once we understand that God has brought us back to relating to Him by faith, we can begin to understand the depths of His grace. He has forgiven all our sins "according to the riches of His grace" (Eph. 1:7), and "where sin increased, grace abounded all the more" (Rom. 5:20). It is "by grace you have been saved through faith; and that not of yourselves, it is the gift of God" (Eph. 2:8). Everything that God has done to forgive our sins and save us He has done by His grace. But grace does not stop there.

Remember, the entire motivation for everything God does is so that we can receive His life. This is the reason why Jesus came. He came that we may have life, and have it abundantly (John 10:10). He spoke to this purpose throughout His ministry. Listen to what Jesus said:

- "For just as the Father has life in Himself, even so He gave to the Son also to have life in Himself" (John 5:26).

- "You search the Scriptures because you think that in them you have eternal life; it is these that testify about Me; and you are unwilling to come to Me so that you may have life" (John 5:39-40).

- "For this is the will of My Father, that everyone who beholds the Son and believes in Him will have eternal life, and I Myself will raise him up on the last day" (John 6:40).

- "...and I give eternal life to them, and they will never perish; and no one will snatch them out of My hand" (John 10:28).

- Jesus said to him, "I am the way, and the truth, and the life; no one comes to the Father but through Me" (John 14:6).

- "This is eternal life, that they may know You, the only true God, and Jesus Christ whom You have sent" (John 17:3).

John himself told us, "In Him was life, and the life was the light of men" (John 1:4) and that "whoever believes will in

Him have eternal life" (John 3:15). He summarized his entire gospel with these words:

> ...but these have been written so that you may believe that Jesus is the Christ, the Son of God; and that believing you may have life in His name (John 20:31).

All of this is leading us to the essence of grace. Paul made it clear when he said that all "those who receive the abundance of grace and of the gift of righteousness will reign *in life through the One, Jesus Christ*" (Rom. 5:17) and that "grace would reign through righteousness *to eternal life through Jesus Christ* our Lord" (Rom. 5:21). Eternal life is not just a reference to something that we receive after we die. Grace connects us to life now! Eternal life is the *quality* of God's life that we experience in the present and it continues for all of eternity. This is why Jesus was resurrected from the grave. He became the "firstborn" from the dead (Col. 1:18; Rom. 8:29) so that He would become a "life-giving spirit" (1 Cor. 15:45). This is the work of God's grace for all of mankind. This is why grace is a foreign concept in the Old Testament. Jesus had to die and be raised by the power of an "indestructible life" (Heb. 7:16) so that He could be the giver of life to all who believe!

I think some of us believe grace is just a mysterious power God gives us at times to cope in life. I am reminded of Luke Skywalker in the old Star Wars movies. In the heat of battle, he always hears the voice of his mentor, Obi-Wan Kenobi, in his mind saying in an ominous voice, "Luke, use the force." This is how a lot of us see grace. We think it is a "force" that is given to help us in times of need.

Paul saw the grace of God as the very practical means by which he lived his life. It was not just something that God gave him to cope with his challenging circumstances. It is true that when he was struggling with the thorn in his flesh the Lord Jesus told him, "My grace is sufficient for you, for power is perfected in weakness" (2 Cor. 12:9). But notice what Paul said at the end of that verse: "I will rather boast about my weaknesses, so that *the power of Christ may dwell in me*" (2 Cor. 12:9). There is the grace! It is the power of Christ's life dwelling in Paul.

I love what Paul said in 1 Corinthians 15:10:

> But by the grace of God I am what I am, and
> His grace toward me did not prove vain; but I
> labored even more than all of them, yet not I, but
> the grace of God with me.

Paul had a full revelation of what grace is. He knew it was *by grace* that he was anything; that the *grace toward* him was effective; and that it was the *grace with* him that accomplished everything. Grace connects us to the very life of Christ, and the whole reason Jesus came was so that we could have life. We must stay focused on this one fact. God wants to give us His life and the way He does this is by grace (Eph. 2:8-9; Rom. 5:21; Titus 3:7).

Paul and Peter wrote fifteen of the twenty-one epistles in the New Testament. (The epistles are the letters that the apostles wrote to the New Testament churches after Pentecost.) Every single one of these letters have a greeting which was common to the writing style of that time. In the greeting of each one of these letters, Paul and Peter included the words "grace and peace." Paul often said, "...grace and peace to you from God our Father and the Lord Jesus Christ" (Rom. 1:7; 1 Cor. 1:3; 2 Cor. 1:2). Is it by coincidence that all these letters start with a reminder of grace and peace to their readers? I don't think so. Paul said in Romans 5:1-2:

> Therefore, having been justified by faith, we have peace with God through our Lord Jesus Christ, through whom also we have obtained our introduction by faith into this grace in which we stand; and we exult in hope of the glory of God.

Paul knew that because of the grace of God we have peace. Peace comes when we know that we are in a right relationship (i.e., justified) with God, and the only way to be in a right relationship with God is by His grace. If we believe that our standing before God is connected to our performance through works, we will never experience peace. The grace of God has removed any requirement for us to perform to gain His approval. God's approval of us is through the grace that He gives us through Jesus Christ. This removes an enormous burden off of us and brings us peace. Without grace there is no peace. We find our peace because we have been justified by faith and we "exult in hope of the glory of God" which is "Christ in you, the hope of glory" (Col. 1:27)!

Grace is not just a way to describe God's attitude or disposition toward us. If we see grace this way, we tend to speak of it in similar terms in our relationships with one another. We talk about "showing grace" or "giving grace" to someone. When we talk like this, we diminish what grace really is in our thinking. The Bible never speaks in terms of people giving grace to others. Only once does it connect grace to our actions. That is when Paul said, "Let your speech always be with grace, as though seasoned with salt, so that you will know how you should respond to each person" (Col. 4:6). When it comes to our interactions with others, Paul also tells us,

> So, as those who have been chosen of God, holy and beloved, put on a heart of compassion, kindness, humility, gentleness and patience; bearing with one another, and forgiving each other, whoever has a complaint against anyone; just as the Lord forgave you, so also should you. Beyond all these things put on love, which is the perfect bond of unity (Col. 3:12-14).

All of these are beautiful qualities of the character of God that should come across in our interactions with one another. We can say they all fall under the category of being "gracious." When we say someone is gracious, we mean that they exhibit these types of qualities in their interaction with other people. We should all endeavor to be gracious people. To reflect these character traits is to reflect the character of God. But the Bible does not instruct us to give grace to one another. This is impossible because only God can give grace.

The reason why only God can impart grace is because grace is God giving us Himself. Grace is not *something*—it is *Someone*! When we first believe in Christ, we receive the abundance of grace and the gift of God's life. From that point on, we stand in the grace (Rom. 5:2) and focus our faith on His life within (Gal. 2:20; Col. 2:6-7). (We will look at this in more detail in Chapter 4 on Faith.) Our responsibility is to acknowledge and receive God's grace at all times and allow it to operate in and through us. This is the essence of the Christian life.

I love the fact that through grace God is constantly providing us with His life. He is living in us. We have the ability to respond to the supply of His life on a daily basis. Whatever situation we find ourselves in, His grace is present and it is enough (2 Cor. 12:9).

If you attempt to live without this truth deeply rooted within you, you will fall into the trap of trying to live the Christian life in your own strength. You will not have a deep appreciation and awareness that by grace God has given you the greatest gift of all—the life of Christ in you, the hope of glory.

Encountering the Truth

Truth: Grace is the continual reality of the life of Christ in you so that you can experience His life living in you, through you, as you.

Faith Declaration: I have received from the fullness of Jesus, grace upon grace, and as I receive the abundance of grace and of the gift of righteousness, I will reign in life through the One, Jesus Christ (Rom. 5:17).

Walking in the Truth

As you walk through each day, choose to acknowledge God's grace in your life. Set your attention on the truth that through the grace of Jesus Christ, His life in you is sufficient for every situation you will face. Live in the awareness that His life in you supplies you with everything you need. Because of grace, His life is dwelling in you and you can experience Him living His life through you every day!

Think about a practical area of your life such as a relationship, situation at work, or a personal challenge. Choose to receive His grace in that specific place in your life and ask Jesus to provide His life in you and through you in that area.

4

FAITH

For I am not ashamed of the gospel, for it is the power of God for salvation to everyone who believes, to the Jew first and also to the Greek. For in it the righteousness of God is revealed from faith to faith; as it is written, "but the righteous man shall live by faith."

~ Romans 1:16-17

I have been crucified with Christ; and it is no longer I who live, but Christ lives in me; and the life which I now live in the flesh I live by faith in the Son of God, who loved me and gave Himself up for me.

~ Galatians 2:20

If grace is the gift of God giving us His life, then faith is the way we receive it. Faith must be at the center of any discussion about the Christian life. When we consider that "without faith it is impossible to please God, for he who comes to God must believe that He is and that He is a rewarder of those who seek Him" (Heb. 11:6), we clearly see that faith is completely necessary. It is non-negotiable. We are called "believers" because we have faith. Faith has always been and will always be the foundation of how we are meant to relate to God. Our ability to exercise faith sets us apart in all of God's creation. He created us with the capacity to express faith toward Him.

I am sure you agree that faith is necessary to being a Christian. Even so, it is still possible to get stuck at a basic understanding of faith and miss the essential truth of what it really means to "live by faith" (Hab. 2:4; Rom. 1:17). Over the years it has helped me to understand faith in three practical ways: (1) faith for salvation; (2) faith for receiving; and (3) faith for living. This does not mean I believe there are different "faiths." There is only "one faith" (Eph. 4:5), but it helps to look at different ways that faith is active in our lives.

You have probably heard the term "saving faith." This comes from Ephesians 2:8-9 where Paul said,

> For by grace you have been *saved through faith*;
> and that not of yourselves, it is the gift of God;
> not as a result of works, so that no one may boast.

We are saved by grace through our faith response to the gospel. Paul said, "...if you confess with your mouth Jesus as Lord, and believe in your heart that God raised Him from the dead, you will be saved" (Rom. 10:9). These verses are talking about our initial faith in the Lord Jesus Christ. Paul called this our "introduction by faith into this grace in which we stand" (Rom. 5:2). Our initial faith response is how we begin our relationship with God. But this only marks the beginning of the rest of our life as a Christian. There is much more for us to understand about faith.

After we begin our relationship with God, we grow in our faith. Our faith needs to become part of our daily life. This means we start learning to trust God in the very practical areas of life. I call this "faith for receiving." God wants us to trust Him for everything we need. We learn to rely on Him for the basic necessities of life (see Matt. 6:25-34). Living in faith should be the normal way for us to live. It means we believe God and have peace that He knows what we need and is able to provide for us in His time and in His way. This is something that my wife and I have been intentional about in our lives over the years, and we have learned that God is faithful in every way.

Trusting God for His provision in any area of our lives should not become the main focus of our faith walk. It is easy to fall into the trap of focusing too much of our energy on believing God for things. It is possible to see faith simply as a tool that we use to get things. We presume that if we simply have enough faith for anything we will eventually receive it from God. This is what I call an "overdeveloped faith" and it can become problematic in a couple of ways.

First, an overdeveloped faith usually has man at its center. There is no doubt that God can and does give us things in response to our faith. We see this over and over in the gospels as Jesus worked miracles. He often told people they had received because of their faith (Matt. 9:22, 29; 15:28; Mark 5:34; 10:52; Luke 7:50; 8:48; 17:19). However, this does not mean that we can simply have faith for anything we want and expect God to do it. Often times we can let our own desires for something dictate our faith. James said, "You ask and do not receive, because you ask with wrong motives, so that you may spend it on your pleasures" (James 4:3). God can see right through the intentions of your heart and He is always more concerned about the condition of your heart than He is about just giving you what you want (see Heb. 4:12; 1 Cor. 4:5). He will work in your life to expose wrong attitudes and bring you into greater dependence on Him. If He simply gave you everything you had faith for, you would never truly need Him. God desires for you to need Him for who He is more than using Him for what He can give you.

Secondly, an overdeveloped faith can neglect the necessity of hearing God's word for our lives. There is a simple but often overlooked principle. "Faith comes from hearing, and hearing by the word of Christ" (Rom. 10:17). This means that before we can have faith we must first hear. This applies to every area of life. We are not able to even come into a relationship with God by faith unless we first hear the word of Christ speaking to our hearts. The same is true as we continue to grow in our relationship with God. We need to first hear His word spoken to us, and when we hear His word, we can respond and believe Him by faith.

There is no limit to what God is able to speak to your heart. Some of the things He speaks may be very hard for you to believe at first, but once you have the assurance that you have heard Him you will have the faith to believe Him. The problem comes when you are not sure you have heard His word and you choose to start believing anyway. This is when your faith can slip into presumption. You need to learn to exercise your faith toward what you know God has spoken and leave the other things behind if you are not sure you have heard Him.

Faith for salvation and faith for receiving are both necessary in the life of every Christian. However, there is a much deeper understanding of living by faith that God wants to give us.

One of the most basic—yet revolutionary—truths about the Christian life is that we were never meant to live it in our own strength. Yes, that's correct! You and I cannot live the Christian life on our own. We just saw in the previous chapter that God provides His grace to do for us what we cannot do for ourselves. This truth should penetrate our lives at the most practical level.

Paul said,

> I have been crucified with Christ; and it is no longer I who live, but Christ lives in me; and the life which I now live in the flesh I live by faith in the Son of God, who loved me and gave Himself up for me (Gal. 2:20).

Paul did not see himself as the one who was alive and living his life any longer. Instead, it was Christ who lived in him and the life which Paul lived he lived *by faith in the Son of God*. This is a profound statement and it is a huge shift in perspective. Before the Lord helped me to see this incredible truth, I thought that the Christian life was something that I needed to do in my own strength and through my own efforts.

I remember the WWJD trend that became popular among Christians in the 1990s. The idea was that Christians would wear a bracelet that had the initials WWJD on them. These letters were an acronym for What Would Jesus Do? The idea was that you would ask yourself this question in every situation. You would then try to act the same way you thought Jesus would act if He was in the same setting.

I don't think the WWJD idea is necessarily a bad one, but it is completely different than living by faith. According to Paul, the Christian life is not lived by trying to figure out what Jesus would do if He was in the same situation as us. The truth is Jesus is literally living His life through us. He wants to naturally express His life at every moment in and through our lives. The only way this happens is through our faith and total dependence on Him. Do you see the difference?

Here is my personal translation of Galatians 2:20:

> I (my sinful self that used to live as the old man) have been crucified with Christ (that old part of me was actually in Christ when he died on the cross and I died with Him when He died); and it is no longer I (my sinful self that used to live as the old man) who live, but Christ who lives in me (in order to animate my life by His life inside of me); and the life which I now live in the flesh (my natural life in this world) I live by faith in the Son of God (which means that every day and every moment I can possibly be aware of, I trust that He is living His life in Me to do, act, and speak so that He literally manifests His life through me), who loved me and gave Himself up for me (He does this for me because He loves me and purchased every right to my life).

God actually intends for Jesus to *be* your life. He never meant for you to try hard to live the Christian life or even to act like Jesus. Jesus lives in your body by His Spirit in order to be your very source of life.

These verses all communicate this truth. Take time to read them and think about what they are saying.

- But we have this treasure in earthen vessels, so that the surpassing greatness of the power will be of God and not from ourselves (2 Cor. 4:7).

- ... always carrying about in the body the dying of Jesus, so that the life of Jesus also may be manifested in our body. For we who live are constantly being delivered over to death for Jesus' sake, so that the life of Jesus also may be manifested in our mortal flesh (2 Cor. 4:10-11).

- For to me, to live is Christ and to die is gain (Phil. 1:21).

- And He has said to me, "My grace is sufficient for you, for power is perfected in weakness." Most gladly, therefore, I will rather boast about my weaknesses, so that the power of Christ may dwell in me (2 Cor. 12:9).

- I have been crucified with Christ; and it is no longer I who live, but Christ lives in me; and the life which I now live in the flesh I live by faith in the Son of God, who loved me and gave Himself up for me (Gal. 2:20).

- For you have died and your life is hidden with Christ in God. When Christ, who is our life, is revealed, then you also will be revealed with Him in glory (Col. 3:3-4).

This gives a whole new meaning to living by faith. It's not just about trusting God to provide for your needs. Living by faith is trusting Jesus to live His life in and through you. This is why you need to trust and believe (i.e., have faith) that Jesus is living His life in and through you every day. As you rely completely on Him and submit to His life in you by faith, He will literally begin to manifest His life in you and you will begin to experience His life living through you (2 Cor. 4:10-12).

This brings us back to my testimony in Chapter 1 about my marriage. The Lord helped me to understand this principle. I started putting my faith in Jesus to live through me as Stephanie's husband. And it worked. Jesus is alive in me and He is a great husband!

I never enjoyed tests in school, but we all know they are one of those inevitable things that we must do. There is also a test for us as believers that we need to take. This is a test to determine if we understand the essence of faith. Paul told the believers in Corinth:

> Test yourselves to see if you are *in the faith*;
> examine yourselves! Or do you not recognize
> this about yourselves, that *Jesus Christ is in you*
> —unless indeed you fail the test? (2 Cor. 13:5).

The test you need to take is the test that determines whether or not you are "in the faith." This test is quite simple because it consists of only one question. The question is "Do you know that Jesus Christ is in you?" The answer to this question will determine whether you pass or fail the test. If your answer is "Yes," you are in the faith and you pass the test. If your answer is "No," you are not in the faith and you fail the test. To know that you are in the faith simply means that you know, believe, and trust that Jesus is in you to live

His life through you. This is what it means to live by faith and this is what it means to be a Christian.

This is the most practical aspect of living the Christian life. Jesus is in you to live His life through you. As you trust Him to do this, He conforms you into His image. All you need to do is continually believe that Jesus is your life. The more you believe this truth, the more you experience the reality of His life in you. When God sees your faith and dependence on Jesus, He begins transforming your life. You are being conformed to the image of Jesus and this is amazing! Your attitudes, thoughts, motives, and actions begin to change. This is the miracle of the Christian life. God is actually "at work in you, both to will and to work for His good pleasure" (Phil. 2:13).

One of my favorite verses that helps me understand my faith in Jesus is Colossians 2:6-7. Paul said,

> Therefore as you have received Christ Jesus the Lord, so walk in Him, having been firmly rooted and now being built up in Him and established *in your faith* just as you were instructed, and overflowing with gratitude.

The way we walk in Christ Jesus is the same way we receive Him. "Walking" is a metaphor that describes the process of living the Christian life. We know that the only way to receive Christ Jesus into our lives is by faith—faith for salvation. There is nothing that we can do to be saved other than to have faith in Jesus. And there is nothing that we can do to live the Christian life other than to have faith in Jesus.

I am always perplexed that we are willing to preach the simple gospel message of salvation and tell people all they need to do to be saved is believe; but then we turn right around after they are saved and tell them all the things they need to do to live the Christian life! This is why so many Christians experience burn out, frustration, discouragement, and eventually "backslide." They simply cannot meet all the demands of being a Christian by trying to do all the right things in their own strength. They haven't heard the whole story. The same way you receive Jesus is the same way you walk in Him. And the only way to walk in Him is by faith.

Your understanding of faith must go to the deepest level of complete trust in Christ in you. The essence of your life is to "learn Christ" by hearing Him and "being taught in Him, just as truth is in Jesus" (Eph. 4:20-21). This happens as you focus your faith on Him, believe that He is your life, and trust Him to live through you each and every day.

Encountering the Truth
Truth: Living by faith means to trust in the life of Jesus within you to live in you, through you, as you.

Faith Declaration: I have been crucified with Christ; and it is no longer I who live, but Christ who lives in me; and the life which I now live in the flesh I live by faith in the Son of God, who loved me and gave Himself up for me (Gal. 2:20).

Walking in the Truth
Direct your faith today to the truth that Jesus Christ lives in you. Trust that Christ will live through you in every situation and circumstance. If there is a specific relationship or situation you are aware of in your life that you recognize you struggle to act, speak, or think in a way that brings life, trust by faith that Jesus is living through you in that situation or circumstance. Christ, who is your life, will do through you what you are unable to do in your own strength or effort.

5

RIGHTEOUSNESS

He made Him who knew no sin to be sin on our behalf, so that we might become the righteousness of God in Him.

~ 2 Corinthians 5:21

And that you be renewed in the spirit of your mind, and put on the new self, which in the likeness of God has been created in righteousness and holiness of the truth.

~ Ephesians 4:23

On October 31, 1517, Martin Luther nailed his Ninety-five Theses on the church door at Wittenberg, Germany. His actions on that day set in motion what became historically known as the Protestant Reformation. At the very center of the Reformation was the debate concerning justification by faith and the righteousness of God. While most of us cannot articulate all the nuances of these events in the history of the church, I assure you we've all been deeply impacted by them. The theological doctrines that emerged from this time period have influenced the way Christians have thought about God for the past 500 years. You and I are included, and many things we believe about salvation by faith, justification, and righteousness have been shaped by the opinions of the great Reformers like Martin Luther and John Calvin.

Righteousness is one of the most common themes in the Bible. The biblical writers mention righteousness over 300 times. It is the one term that communicates the essence of God's character more than any other. If "God is love" (1 John 4:16) is the most accurate statement about *who* God is, then the "righteousness of God" (Rom. 3:21) is the most accurate statement of *what* He is like.

Theology often has a way of making things more complicated rather than making them more clear. Theologians have debated for centuries over the definition of righteousness and the role it plays in the relationship between God and man. Sometimes I adhere to the "Theology for Dummies" approach—just keep it practical and to the point. That is my perspective when it comes to a topic like righteousness.

Most definitions for righteousness place a strong emphasis on morality. According to these definitions, righteousness is the aspect of God's character that reflects His moral standard. When we view righteousness this way, we focus on the moral standard that God desires for us to attain to in our attitudes and actions.

There is definitely a moral element to righteousness, but I don't believe it is the primary focus. The word literally means "to be right or just." The very first time "righteousness" appears in the Bible is in Abraham's interaction with God. Abraham "believed in the Lord; and He reckoned it to him as righteousness" (Gen. 15:6). The interaction between Abraham and God had nothing to do with Abraham's moral behavior. He simply believed God and God declared him "right." His "rightness" or "righteousness" was based on his faith and not his actions.

There is a reason why we have trouble seeing righteousness from God's perspective. Our thinking has been deeply tainted by sin. Sin entered into the world through Adam and Eve eating from the tree of the knowledge of good and evil (Rom. 5:12). When this happened, their total perspective became defined in terms of morality, which is nothing more than the principles concerning the distinction between good and evil—right and wrong. God never created man and woman to live with this capacity. That is why it was the one thing that God forbid them to do. He knew the devastating effects it would have on mankind. But because of love, God gave Adam and Eve the freedom to choose. The rest is history!

God never intended for our relationship with Him to be based on our moral activity and our ability to do the right thing. He wants our relationship with Him to be based on life. I have already pointed out that from the very beginning of time, God wanted to share His life with us so we could live in a safe and secure relationship with Him. Ever since things went so terribly wrong in the garden, God began moving towards His ultimate purpose of bringing mankind back to where he could participate in His life.

This is such an essential truth in our relationship with God. All God ever wanted was to be in a life-giving relationship with mankind. He was never going to make our performance the foundation of our relationship with Him. But, when Adam and Eve made the decision to eat from the wrong tree, it indelibly changed them and the way they related to God. And when God gave them freedom to choose, He also worked in the context of their decision.

This is a profound truth that helps us to see how we can easily misunderstand righteousness. God chooses to allow our decisions to shape the way we relate to Him. He never changes, but the way we perceive Him does. Often times—I dare say most of the time—we perceive Him in ways that are not the most accurate.

For example, God never intended the children of Israel to have a king. But they insisted that they wanted a king like all the other nations around them and God gave them one (1 Sam. 8:4-9). From that point on, it seems like throughout the rest of the Old Testament God is "pro king." God's only desire was for Israel to look to Him as their king and trust in Him to protect and provide for them. But He allowed them to have a king and allowed their perception of Him as "pro king" to be shaped by their own decision.

David said,

> With the kind You
>   show Yourself kind;
> With the blameless
>   You show Yourself
>   blameless;
> With the pure You show
>   Yourself pure,

    And with the crooked
        You show Yourself
        astute (Psalm 18:25-26).

This is how God relates to us and it affects the way we understand righteousness. When Adam and Eve chose to relate to God on the basis of good and evil, right and wrong, God agreed to relate to them in that way. But was this really the way God wanted the relationship to work?

I think by now you probably know the answer to that question. The answer is "No." God wanted our relationship with Him to be characterized by life. He wanted to give us His life so that we could enjoy a perfect relationship with Him forever. This would have been the ultimate place of right standing with God—sharing in His life together with Him. Fear was never meant to be part of our relationship with God, only deep security that comes from the knowledge that God is pleased with us. But if we believe that our relationship with Him is based on doing the right thing, we will always struggle with fear because we will never know if we are doing well enough or not. When we know and believe that God never intended for us to relate to Him through our performance, we begin to understand righteousness from a different perspective.

Paul has more to say about the righteousness of God than any other biblical writer, and most of what he says about it is in the book of Romans. The book of Romans, more than any other, is Paul's treatise of the gospel. He said, "For I am not ashamed of the gospel, for it is the power of God for salvation to everyone who believes" and "in it the righteousness of God is revealed" (Rom. 1:16-17).

Romans 3:21-26 contain some of the most important truth about the righteousness of God:

> But now apart from the Law the righteousness of God has been *manifested*, being witnessed by the Law and the Prophets, even the righteousness of God through faith in Jesus Christ for all those who believe; for there is no distinction; for all have sinned and fall short of the glory of God, being justified as a gift by His grace through the redemption which is in Christ Jesus; whom God displayed publicly as a propitiation in His blood through faith. This was to *demonstrate* His righteousness, because in the forbearance of God He passed over the sins previously committed; for the demonstration, I say, of His righteousness at the present time, so that He would be just and the justifier of the one who has faith in Jesus.

There are two important things to notice about the righteousness of God in these verses. First, it is *manifested* through faith in Jesus Christ. Second, God *demonstrated* His righteousness at the cross when Jesus shed His blood for the forgiveness of all sins. This means that God made His righteousness visible and displayed it for all to see through the sacrifice of Jesus.

Paul says that when God chose to show His righteousness at the cross *and* when He chose to forgive all sins (even those committed before Jesus died), He did the right thing because Jesus' perfect sacrifice paid the debt in full. God showed His righteousness. This makes God "just and the justifier of the one who has faith in Jesus" (Rom. 3:26). Paul is telling us that the very actions of God in the gospel events show us that God is right in what He does, and He is the one who has the right to declare us righteous based on our faith in what He has done.

Paul then unfolds this wonderful truth in the next two chapters of Romans. The foundation of his presentation is built on the profound difference between the choice Adam made and the choice Jesus made. Adam (and Eve) chose independence from God and ate from the wrong tree. As the result of Adam's actions, death was released upon all mankind!

But Jesus made a different choice. He chose to live completely dependent on the Father and to ultimately lay down His life as the perfect sacrifice for the sins of the world. His willingness to be the final sacrifice for sin is what Paul described as the "one act of righteousness." He said,

> For if by the transgression of the one, death reigned through the one, much more those who receive the abundance of grace and of the gift of righteousness will reign in life through the One, Jesus Christ. So then as through one transgression there resulted condemnation to all men, even so through one act of righteousness there resulted justification of life to all men (Rom. 5:17-18).

It is imperative that we understand this extraordinary truth (see the diagram on the next page). First, there is nothing we did to be condemned before God. It was through Adam's act of disobedience that *all* are condemned. In the same way, there is nothing we can do to be justified before God. We are justified because of what Jesus has already done through His one act of righteousness.

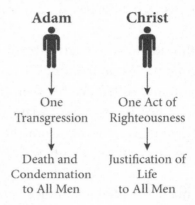

Adam   Christ

One   One Act of
Transgression   Righteousness

Death and   Justification of
Condemnation   Life
to All Men   to All Men

Second—and this is a very important thing to see—Paul said that "through one act of righteousness there resulted *justification of life to all men*" (Rom. 5:18). At first glance this statement may sound like Paul is saying everyone is justified. This kind of interpretation has led some people to promote universalism. This is the belief that all people will be saved regardless of whether they choose to believe or not. But this is not what Paul is saying. There is a difference between the justification of life "to all men" and the justification "of all men." He says that the righteous act of Jesus on the cross resulted in justification of life *to* all men. He does not say it resulted in all men being justified. He is telling us that God has done everything necessary through the death of Jesus to bring about justification of life to everyone. He then offers this justification to all who will receive it by faith. God has done everything on His part to justify all people, but we have to receive the free gift through faith (Rom. 5:17). When we do, it results in righteousness—being right with God.

Now that we know God has demonstrated His righteousness through the death of Jesus on the cross and has extended justification of life to us through this act of righteousness, we can make the final application to how righteousness impacts our lives on a personal level. Paul highlighted this most powerfully in 2 Corinthians 5:21. He said, "He made Him who knew no sin to be sin on our behalf, so that we might become the righteousness of God in Him." Notice these two words, "made" and "become." Paul says God "made" Jesus, who did not know sin, to know sin on our behalf. Jesus did not become sin. The original Greek in this verse does not have the words "to be." God did not make Jesus "to be" sin, He made Him who knew no sin "to know" or "to experience" it on our behalf.

But when it comes to what God did for us, Paul said something astounding. He literally said we "become" the righteousness of God in Christ. This is a completely different word in this part of the verse. The word "become" in the Greek means "to come into being." It is the same word John used when he talked about how Jesus created all things. He said, "All things came into being through Him, and apart from Him nothing came into being that has come into being" (John 1:3). This word means that something has come into being that did not exist beforehand. Paul is saying that we, who were not righteous, actually become the righteousness of God in Christ. What an incredible truth!

Jesus did what He did on the cross so you could be righteous. Receive this wonderful truth by faith and "be renewed in the spirit of your mind, and put on the new self, which in the likeness of God has been created in *righteousness* and holiness of the truth" (Eph. 4:23-24).

Paul put it another way when he said,

> But by His doing you are in Christ Jesus,
> who became to us wisdom from God,
> and righteousness and sanctification, and
> redemption, so that, just as it is written, "Let him
> who boasts, boast in the Lord" (1 Cor. 1:30).

You are not in the process of becoming righteous by doing more right things. Christ is your righteousness and when you are in Him you are righteous. There is a big difference between you becoming righteous based on how you perform and being righteous based on the fact that you are in Christ!

As we progress through the next few chapters, it will become clear how God has made perfect provision for you through all that Jesus Christ has done. Believing the reality of your righteousness in Christ is foundational to you living in the fullness of your right standing with God. He has made you righteous so that you can have the peace that comes in knowing beyond any doubt that God is pleased with you in the deepest possible way. God has made you righteous based on what Christ has done and not on what you do. It is based on His character, not yours. You are accepted and approved because of His righteousness that He has freely shared with you.

Encountering the Truth

Truth: You are the righteousness of God in Christ Jesus.

Faith Declaration: I believe that God has made me completely righteous, and I know that there is nothing I can do to be righteous and earn God's approval. Because of my faith in Jesus, I am in Christ, who is my righteousness. I am righteous!

🚶 *Walking in the Truth*

Each day meditate on what it means to be righteous. You are in a right relationship with God and He is completely satisfied and pleased with you because of your faith in Christ. Whenever you feel like God is not happy with you, choose to believe the truth that He has made you righteous. Remind yourself that you do not need to strive or perform for God's approval. Rest in the truth that you are accepted in the Beloved today!

6

FORGIVENESS

If you, Lord, should mark iniquities, O Lord, who could stand? But there is forgiveness with You, that You may be feared.
~ Psalms 130:3-4

"Therefore let it be known to you, brethren, that through Him forgiveness of sins is proclaimed to you, and through Him everyone who believes is freed from all things, from which you could not be freed through the Law of Moses."
~ Acts 13:38-39

You have probably heard the saying, "If it sounds too good to be true, it probably is." We all grew up hearing this and we developed a general skepticism towards things that sound too good to be true, mostly because we don't want to experience too much disappointment in life. This is a common response from people when I share about God's forgiveness. They are skeptical when they hear the truth because it just sounds too good to be true.

Forgiveness is at the very heart of the gospel. David prophetically declared, "How blessed is he whose transgression is forgiven, whose sin is covered!" (Psalm 32:1). Zacharias, the father of John the Baptist, prophesied these words about John after his birth:

> "And you, child, will be
>   called the prophet of
>   the Most High;
> For you will go on
>   before the Lord to
>   prepare His ways;
> To give to His people the
>   knowledge of salvation
> By the forgiveness of
>   their sins" (Luke 1:76-77).

When the risen Lord encountered Paul on the road to Damascus, He told Paul He was sending him to the Jews and Gentiles to

> "...open their eyes so that they may turn from darkness to light and from the dominion of Satan to God, that they may receive forgiveness of sins and an inheritance among those who have been sanctified by faith in Me" (Acts 26:18).

Jesus redeemed us through His blood and forgave us of all our sins (Eph. 1:7, Col. 2:13). The message of the gospel is one of forgiveness of sins.

Afer studying what the New Testament writers say about forgiveness, I have developed five statements that summarize what I see as the essence of their teaching on forgiveness. I will use these to guide my discussion. They are:

1. Forgiveness is something that God did long before we were ever born, or ever believed in Jesus.

2. When Jesus died on the cross, God forgave all sins for all time.

3. Since God has forgiven all sins for all time, all your sins—past, present, and future—are already forgiven.

4. After we become a Christian, there is nothing we have to do to get God to forgive us because it is something that He has already done.

5. The sacrifice of Jesus and the forgiveness of our sins removes our consciousness of sin.

Let's take a closer look at each one of these statements in light of what the Scriptures teach about forgiveness.

1. Forgiveness is something that God did long before we were ever born, or ever believed in Jesus.

I like to ask people this question, "On what grounds does God forgive sin?" This simply means what is the reason or justification God has to forgive sins. The answer is that God forgives sins on the grounds that Jesus died on the cross. God forgives all sins based on His Son's obedience to shed His blood and to die. Maybe you haven't ever heard it put this way, so let's take a closer look.

The writer of Hebrews—I am not going to conjecture who that might be—tells us that Jesus Christ is the mediator of a New Covenant. Another word for covenant is testament. Most of us have heard of a "last will and testament." In human terms this is a legal document that communicates a person's final wishes pertaining to their worldly possessions. Wills and testaments can differ in many ways, but there is one fundamental similarity to them all. Nothing in the will and testament happens until the person whose will it is dies.

There is a very important passage of Scripture that explains this truth as it specifically relates to the forgiveness of sins. The writer of Hebrews said,

> For this reason He is the mediator of a new covenant, so that, since a death has taken place for the redemption of the transgressions that were committed under the first covenant, those who have been called may receive the promise of the eternal inheritance. For where a covenant is, *there must of necessity be the death of the one who made it.* For a covenant is valid only when men are dead, for it is never in force while the one who made it lives (Heb. 9:15-17).

Here are two more important differences between the Old Covenant and the New Covenant. First, the New Covenant is better than the Old Covenant (Heb. 8:7, 13). It is better because Jesus was a better priest (Heb. 7:22) and a better sacrifice (Heb. 9:11-14). It was also enacted on better promises (Heb. 8:6).

Second, the New Covenant was much shorter and more concise than the Old Covenant. The Old Covenant refers to the covenant God made with the people of Israel when He gave the Law to Moses in the wilderness. This covenant was conditionally based upon Israel's performance and consisted of 613 commandments. God knew from the very beginning that the children of Israel would forsake Him and never keep this covenant (Deut. 31:16). After hundreds of years of disobedience, God promised that He would make a New Covenant with Israel (Jer. 31:31).

This New Covenant has no conditions and only two features. The writer of Hebrews said,

> "This is the covenant that I will make with them after those days, says the Lord: I will put My laws upon their heart, and on their mind I will write them," He then says, "And their sins and their lawless deeds I will remember no more" (Heb. 10:16-17).

The two features of the New Covenant are:

1. God will put His laws upon our hearts and on our minds.

2. God will forgive our sins and will not remember them anymore.

Now let's go back to the verses about Jesus being the mediator of the New Covenant. The writer is telling us that God knew from His interactions with Israel that people were incapable of keeping any type of agreement with Him. They always failed miserably. This was Israel's ongoing history (Deut. 31:14-18). God decided He would make a new agreement (covenant).

The New Covenant that God made was not between God and man. It was with Himself. God the Father and God the Son entered into an agreement. God decided that He would forgive all the sins of mankind forever. This was the provision of the will and testament—so to speak. But in order for the condition of the will to take place there had to be the death of the one who made it. So, God the Son died.

When Jesus died, the covenant that God issued went into effect. Now for a big question. What role did you and I play in this entire process? The answer is "None!" We were not involved in this process at all. Does it almost sound too good to be true? Well, it gets even better. This is why it is called the gospel, the good news.

When Jesus died, God forgave "all sins for all time" (Heb. 10:12). The reason God forgave sins was because Jesus died. He honored the covenant He made with the Son (Is. 42:6), and when Jesus died, the provision of the covenant went into effect. This is a "once and for all" (Heb. 10:10) event that will never be repeated again. The grounds on which God forgave sins and when He forgave sins are inextricably linked. God forgave sins because Jesus died, and Jesus died almost 2000 years ago. From this fact we know forgiveness is something God did long before we were ever born, or ever believed in Jesus.

2. *When Jesus died on the cross, God forgave all sins for all time.*

Now that we know the grounds upon which God forgave sins and when God forgave sins, let's find out how many sins He forgave. The little diagram on the next page will make it easy to see.

This picture illustrates all of the sins ever committed over the course of human history from "Creation" to the "Return of Christ." We know that there was a specific time in the past

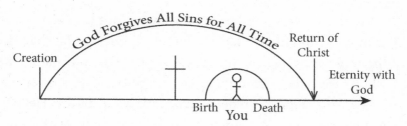

when the first sin was committed by Adam and Eve in the garden of Eden, and we know that there will be a time in the future when sins will end. There are many opinions about what the "end" looks like, but for the sake of our discussion we will just say there will be an end and people will stop committing sins. This means there is actually a finite number of sins committed over the course of humanity. That number is really large, but it is finite because there was a beginning and there will be an end.

We will stay in the book of Hebrews to find out how many sins God forgave. Hebrews 10:11-12 says,

> Every priest stands daily ministering and offering time after time the same sacrifices, which can never take away sins; but He, having offered one sacrifice for sins for all time, sat down at the right hand of God.

These verses make it clear that under the Old Covenant the sacrifices offered were unable to take away sins. But, unlike those sacrifices, Jesus offered Himself as the one sacrifice for sins for all time! That means that the sacrifice of Jesus was enough to remove all the sins ever committed from the beginning of the world until the end. This is one reason why the writer of Hebrews says that Jesus obtained "eternal redemption" (Heb. 9:12). God forgave sins forever!

Redemption is another way of saying forgiveness of sins. Paul said, "In Him we have redemption through His blood, the forgiveness of our trespasses" (Eph. 1:7), and again, "in whom we have redemption, the forgiveness of sins (Col. 1:14). To say God has redeemed us simply means that He has forgiven our sins. Redemption means to "purchase back" or to "gain possession of something in exchange for a payment." This means that God purchased us so that He could gain possession of our lives. When Jesus shed His blood and died on the cross, He paid the price necessary for God to purchase us (Acts 20:28; Rev. 5:9). The shedding of His blood secured the forgiveness of sins (Heb. 9:22). Payment has been made in full so *all* sins have been forgiven.

This is such a beautiful explanation of what God has done through the one act of Jesus offering Himself as the perfect sacrifice. In this one act of obedience by Jesus, God forgave all sins. "Thanks be to God for His indescribable gift!" (2 Cor. 9:15).

3. Since God has forgiven all sins for all time, all your sins— past, present, and future—are already forgiven.

We know the grounds on which God forgave sins, when God forgave sins, and how many sins He forgave. Now let's look at where your sins fit into the story. This may seem obvious, but I have seen many people struggle to make the practical application of this powerful truth.

Take another look at the diagram. You are represented in the diagram by the little person with the small arch over his head. As an analytical person, I like to interpret this diagram in mathematical terms of a set and a subset. A set is a well-defined collection of objects. In this case, the collection of

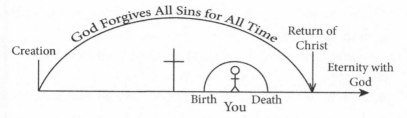

Creation

God Forgives All Sins for All Time

Return of Christ

Eternity with God

Birth   You   Death

objects is all the sins of the world ever committed represented by the large arch. The smaller arch over your life signifies the collection of objects of another set that represents all the sins you will commit during your lifetime. Now for the beauty of the math. The definition of a subset is a set whose collection of objects is also part of another set. And whatever is true for the set is also true for the subset.

From the math we rightly deduce that because God forgave all sins—the set—for all time, He also forgave all your sins—the subset—for all time. You never have to wonder, worry, or hope that your sins are forgiven. God forgave them when Jesus died on the cross.

4. *As Christians, there is nothing we have to do to get God to forgive us because it is something that He has already done.*

The more I share this truth with Christians, the more I realize that there are many believers who think that there is still something they must do to receive God's forgiveness after they become a Christian. This notion comes from different teachings that influence us early in our Christian lives. Some people make God's forgiveness contingent on their emotions. They are only able to experience God's forgiveness to the extent that they feel like He has forgiven them. For example, some think that if they feel guilty and are sorry enough for their sin, then God will be quicker to forgive them. They think their forgiveness depends on the genuineness of their sorrow or repentance.

Others may feel that the severity of their sins makes a difference on when they can expect forgiveness. If the sin is a really "bad" sin then they might have to wait a certain period of time without sinning before they can feel like God has forgiven them. This type of belief leads many Christians to formulate different grades of sins, and the worse the sin the longer they must feel bad before they can feel forgiven.

Some people even believe that their sin causes a separation between them and God. This notion is what led the Catholic church to develop what they call the "seven deadly sins." They believe these sins are so bad that they sever a person from God's grace. They teach that the sins of lust, gluttony, greed, sloth, wrath, envy, and pride are the worst sins that a person can commit and carry with them greater potential punishment, thus making penance more necessary in order to reestablish connection with God.

These types of beliefs are all grounded in an Old Covenant mentality that says we can never be totally confident that we are forgiven because there is always a "reminder of sins" (Heb. 10:3). But the truth is God has already forgiven all sins, so there is nothing that we must do to gain His forgiveness nor is there anything we can do to earn it. (I will go into more detail of this in the next chapter on Confession.) Forgiveness is something that He has already done. God wants us to have full assurance that we are totally forgiven. He wants us to be secure and confident so that we can enjoy continual fellowship with Him no matter what we do. If we feel that God is far away when we sin, this is more discouraging and detrimental in our relationship with Him. God wants us to know that we're forgiven so that if/when we do sin we can "draw near with confidence to the throne of grace, so that we may receive mercy and find grace to help in time of need" (Heb. 4:16).

The apostles help to clarify how forgiveness operates in the life of the believer. Peter and Paul both made a similar statement about forgiveness in their preaching in the book of Acts. Peter said in Acts 10:43, "Of Him all the prophets bear witness that through His name *everyone who believes* in Him receives forgiveness of sins." Paul said in Acts 13:38-39:

> "Therefore let it be known to you, brethren, that through Him forgiveness of sins is proclaimed to you, and through Him *everyone who believes* is freed from all things, from which you could not be freed through the Law of Moses."

In both of these sermons there is a direct correlation between *believing* and *receiving* forgiveness of sins. Peter and Paul understood that God had forgiven all sins, and their job was to proclaim forgiveness of sins wherever they went. This is what it means to preach the gospel. We are actually telling people good news! We are telling them that their sins have already been forgiven. The good news is that God has forgiven them in Christ. To receive His forgiveness, all they have to do is believe.

Jesus said, "He who believes in Him is not judged; he who does not believe has been judged already, because he has not believed in the name of the only begotten Son of God" (John 3:18). This is Jesus' way of saying what Peter and Paul said. If we believe, we personally receive forgiveness for our sins and will not experience judgment. If we do not believe, we do not personally receive forgiveness for our sins and will ultimately be judged. Here is another way of saying it. Heaven (eternity with God) will be full of forgiven people who believed, and hell (separation from God) will be full of forgiven people who did not believe! We will not be judged based on our sins. God has forgiven them all. We will be judged based on whether or not we have faith and believe.

Forgiveness is actually a very rare topic in the apostolic letters of the New Testament. I believe the reason for this is obvious in light of what I have shared so far in this chapter. The apostles knew the truth that God's forgiveness of sins was complete and final at the cross. When they do speak about forgiveness of sins, it is either in the past tense (Eph. 4:32; Col. 2:13; 3:13; 1 John 2:12), or it is something that we already have (Eph. 1:7; Col. 1:14).

Paul only made mention of forgiveness once in Romans when he quoted David from Psalms 32:1 when he said,

> "Blessed are those whose
>   lawless deeds have
>   been forgiven,
> And whose sins have been
>   covered.
> Blessed is the man
>   whose sin the Lord
>   will not take into
>   account" (Rom. 4:7-8).

Otherwise, Paul made no mention of God's forgiveness of sins anywhere else in Romans or in 1 & 2 Corinthians, Galatians, Philippians, 1 & 2 Thessalonians, 1 & 2 Timothy, Titus, and Philemon. Peter made no mention of forgiveness in 1 & 2 Peter. Out of the four books John wrote, 1, 2, & 3 John and Revelation, he only mentioned forgiveness two times (1 John 1:9; 2:12); and James mentioned it only once (James 5:15).

The apostles did not continually speak about the need for forgiveness because they knew it was already done. They knew that once we have received God's amazing forgiveness we can live free to explore more of who we are in Christ.

5. *The sacrifice of Jesus and the forgiveness of our sins removes our consciousness of sin.*

I am always saddened by how many believers have a hyper awareness of their sin. I call this being sin-conscious (Heb. 10:2). If many Christians were honest, they would say that they do indeed have sin in their lives and that they think about it a lot. In fact, they are usually obsessed with the thought of it. They are either constantly focusing on their sin because they want to do everything they can to get free from it and not do it again, or they stumble and are carrying the burden and guilt of the sin they have committed. Either way they end up thinking about it a lot. Many people focus on not sinning, believing if they don't they will automatically do the sin they are working so hard not to do!

Hebrews 9:9 tells us that all the gifts and sacrifices that were offered under the Old Covenant were unable to "make the worshiper perfect in conscience." The sacrifices made under the Old Covenant would have ceased if they would have cleansed the worshipers, and if they were cleansed they would no longer have had a "consciousness of sins" (Heb. 10:2). Instead, the sacrifices they offered were a constant "reminder of sins year after year" (Heb. 10:3). This was a burdensome way to live. But the good news is that the one perfect sacrifice of Jesus put an end to the continual sacrifices that reminded them of their sin. And His sacrifice put an end to us being reminded of our sin.

To have our conscience cleansed does not mean that we ignore sin in our lives. We should always walk as children of Light "trying to learn what is pleasing to the Lord" (Eph. 5:10, 1 Thess. 4:1). The point is that if and when we do fail, we don't have to carry about the guilt and awareness of our wrong. There may be natural consequences that serve to remind us, but there is little we can do about that. However, when it comes to our relationship with God, He does not remember our sins and He doesn't want us to either. This is one of the most beautiful facts about the sacrifice of Jesus. We are completely forgiven and the blood of Jesus removes our consciousness of sin.

On a practical level, most people are conscious of the sins they have committed in the past. We usually don't sit around and think about the sins we are going to do in the future, whether it is later today, two weeks from now, or ten years from now. It is the things we have done in the past that we carry around in our conscience, and God wants to set us free from our awareness of those misdeeds. His forgiveness has released us completely and we can enjoy our freedom without any guilt or shame. This is the path to abundant life!

The truth is that God has forgiven all our sins and when we know that we are completely forgiven, it sets us free from always thinking about our sin. In my own personal journey, this was one of the most difficult things for me to accept because everything in my natural mind told me this couldn't be true. But through the process of accepting the truth, believing it, and being renewed in the spirit of my mind, I have come into a deeper measure of freedom. This is such a wonderful way to live life and I am passionate to share it with people every chance I get.

One last practical note on forgiveness is in order before I finish this chapter. You will remember from the very start of this book my focus has been on the essential truth that is based completely on what God has done for us through Jesus Christ. But any discussion on forgiveness would be incomplete without mentioning the importance of forgiving others when they do wrong to us and asking others for forgiveness when we wrong them for any reason. Paul said clearly that we are to forgive one another, "just as God in Christ also has forgiven you" (Eph. 4:32; Col. 3:13). Paul's whole attitude here reflects the truth that due to the fact that God has freely forgiven us in Christ, we should obviously forgive one another in the same way. I have found practically that when people fully understand the forgiveness of God in their lives, it does become easier to forgive others.

We know that there are many ill effects of unforgiveness in our lives like bitterness, judgment, and even physical illness, but God withholding forgiveness from us is not one of them! For God to do that He would have to ignore the shed blood of His Son and the covenant He made with Him, and this is something that He will never do.

Now is a good time to discuss another difference between the Old and New Covenants. I have already touched on the covenants, but I want to go a bit deeper because it is important to our understanding of forgiveness, as well as other areas of our relationship with God.

I think many believers struggle in their relationship with God because they stand with one foot in the New Covenant while keeping the other foot in the Old Covenant. This leads to big problems in our belief system, which has a direct impact on how we relate to God.

The New Covenant represents a new and living way that God established through His Son, Jesus Christ. Most every Christian I speak to would agree that there is a New Covenant. However, things become a bit fuzzy if you go further into their understanding of the difference between the two covenants.

Let's look at the difference between the covenants according to the biblical writers. The Old Covenant was based on the letter of the law, but the New Covenant is based on the Spirit (2 Cor. 3:6). The Old Covenant of the letter kills and is a ministry of death, but the New Covenant of the Spirit brings life (2 Cor. 3:6). The Old Covenant was not faultless and required a New Covenant that was effective (Heb. 8:7). The New Covenant made the Old Covenant obsolete (Heb. 8:13). The sacrifices of the Old Covenant could never take away sins (Heb. 10:4, 11), but the blood of the New Covenant (Matt. 26:28) takes away sin (1 John 3:5). The Old Covenant was based on the works of the law, and the New Covenant is based on grace operating through faith (Gal. 3:5). The Old Covenant was based on the conditions of the law that were given to Moses, and the New Covenant is based on grace and truth that was manifested in Jesus Christ (John 1:17).

The New Covenant started when Jesus Christ shed his blood on the cross. This means that while Jesus was alive He was living under the Old Covenant. He was "born under the Law, so that He might redeem those who were under the Law" (Gal. 4:4-5). Jesus Himself said, "I was sent only to the lost sheep of the house of Israel" (Matt. 15:24). We know from the rest of the story that salvation was for the whole world, but during His lifetime Jesus was focusing His attention on the Jews. As the promised Messiah to the Jewish people, Jesus almost exclusively interacted with Jews during His three-year public ministry. This time is recorded for us in the four gospels—Matthew, Mark, Luke, and John.

It is imperative that we understand that the gospel writers were recording the activities of Jesus' life during His time on earth before the New Covenant was in effect. He taught as a Jew who was under the Law, to those who were under the Law. All of what Jesus said to the Jews during His earthly ministry reflected what was true under the Old Covenant.

The vast majority of what is recorded in the gospels is Jesus' interaction with Jews. Only on a couple of occasions does He speak with Gentiles. The woman at the well was a Samaritan (John 4), and the Syrophoenician woman was a Gentile (Matt. 15:21-28; Mark 7:24-30). Jesus also healed the Roman Centurion's servant (Luke 7:2-10) and the royal official's son (John 4:46-54). All of these interactions contain instances where Jesus showed compassion and displayed His miraculous power to heal or to prophecy. However, when it comes to teaching and instruction, with the exception of the woman at the well when He spoke to her about true worship, Jesus only did this with the Jews. We need to always keep this in mind as we read the gospels and seek to understand the truth in what Jesus was saying to His Jewish audience. Then we can discern if and how it applies to us under the New Covenant.

This approach is fundamental to good, responsible Bible study and Scripture interpretation. Taking Scriptures out of context has led to many negative results throughout church history. We don't want to make the same mistakes. Nonetheless, many people still want to take the teachings of Jesus under the Old Covenant and apply them to the New Covenant. This is a sure recipe for disaster. We need to be confident enough in the reality of the New Covenant to admit that even what Jesus says under the Old Covenant does not apply to people living in the New Covenant—this includes you.

Even Jesus had a view toward things that would happen through the inauguration of the New Covenant, but He did not speak about them fully before they happened. He knew that things would only change once He completed what He came to do through His death, burial, and resurrection.

This does not mean that the Scriptures that contain the teachings of Jesus are not inspired! It simply means that they have their proper place in understanding the full process of God in history. We learn about the true character and nature of God through the way Jesus interacted with people in compassion and love. He was full of "grace and truth" (John 1:14) and was the radiance of God's glory and the exact representation of His nature (Heb. 1:3).

This perspective helps us to reconcile what Jesus taught about forgiveness in the "Lord's prayer." Jesus said that we should ask God to forgive our sins as we forgive others and that "if you do not forgive others, then your Father will not forgive your transgressions" (Matt. 6:9-14). This is a very ominous way to live. It puts a strong condition on forgiveness that most of us are unable to bear. But we must understand that for the Jew this type of condition was deeply rooted in their understanding of how God related to them. It would not have come as any surprise for a Jew to hear Jesus explain forgiveness in this way. However, this is not a condition that is carried into the New Covenant. There is no condition on forgiveness in the New Covenant teaching of the apostles. (We will look at this in more detail in the next chapter on Confession.)

Forgiveness is the free gift of God for the whole world as the result of what Jesus has done at the cross. For any who will believe, they receive forgiveness (Acts 10:43; 13:39). Under the New Covenant forgiveness is solely dependent on the shed blood of Jesus!

God knows that in this life we will always have the capacity to sin, and it is for this reason that He has provided forgiveness. It is impossible to out-sin God's forgiveness! But immediately someone will ask the question, "What about the unforgivable sin?" Jesus said,

> "Truly I say to you, all sins shall be forgiven the sons of men, and whatever blasphemies they utter; but whoever blasphemes against the Holy Spirit never has forgiveness, but is guilty of an eternal sin." (Mark 3:28-29; Matt. 12:31-32).

As we will see in Chapter 10, the Spirit's role is to convict non-Christians of their sin of unbelief. If they will listen and agree with the Spirit, have faith and confess, they will receive forgiveness. If they ignore the Spirit's conviction—this is what it means to blaspheme the Spirit—they cannot receive forgiveness because they do not believe. That is why the sin of unbelief cannot be forgiven. God is looking for faith and He gives us the freedom to choose.

As children of God, we continually enjoy God's forgiveness. It is something that is always present in our lives. No matter what we do, we are already forgiven. In fact, we cannot *not* be forgiven.

I know there is an automatic response to this truth that you may have when you hear it for the first time. You might say, "I cannot just sin all I want and God will always forgive me." The truth of the matter is you can and He already has. As wonderful as this truth is, it is only one aspect of all the truth. There is still another aspect that leads to deep transformation and true freedom as you experience victory over sin patterns. (We will discuss this truth in Chapter 8 on Sin.) For now, this essential truth about forgiveness needs to go deep into your thinking as you believe it by faith. While it may sound too good to be true, it really is true. You need to have a bold faith to believe what God is telling you about His forgiveness so that you can enjoy the depths of what He has done for you through Jesus Christ.

Encountering the Truth

Truth: When Jesus died on the cross, God forgave all sins for all time; therefore, all your sins—past, present, and future—are forgiven.

Faith Declaration: All of my sins have been forgiven and I can live in total freedom and peace with God. I will draw near with confidence to the throne of grace to receive mercy and find grace to help in my time of need.

Walking in the Truth

Begin each day thanking God for His complete work of forgiveness through the shed blood of Jesus. Believe that all your sins—past, present, and future—were forgiven at the cross. When you do anything that you believe is sinful, thank God for His forgiveness and believe that He wants you to draw near. If you are plagued by a consciousness of your sin, confess and believe the truth of God's forgiveness and the blood of Jesus in your life. He does not want you to live in guilt and condemnation.

7

CONFESSION

If we confess our sins, He is faithful and righteous to forgive us our sins and to cleanse us from all unrighteousness.

~ 1 John 1:9

Therefore, confess your sins to one another, and pray for one another so that you may be healed. The effective prayer of a righteous man can accomplish much.

~ James 5:16

Thomas Dewar was a Scottish Baron and distiller of fine Scottish whiskey at the turn of the twentieth century. He is quoted as saying, "An honest confession is good for the soul, but bad for the reputation." It's a funny anecdote that reveals the influence confession has had over time. The history of confession in the church is an interesting one influenced mostly by the practices of the Roman Catholics that began sometime in the 5th century and ultimately became common practice in the 11th century. The decision of the fourth Lateran Council in 1215 established the rule that every Christian should confess to a priest at least once a year.

The common practice of confession in the church is not completely congruent with what the Bible teaches about confession. In the Old Testament confession of sin is mentioned only a few times. In the Mosaic Law, there is one instance where the worshipper is to "confess that in which he has sinned" (Lev. 5:5; Num. 5:7). Aaron is instructed to lay his hands on the head of the sacrificial goat and "confess over it all the iniquities of the sons of Israel" (Lev. 16:21). And twice in the Psalms David mentions confessing his transgression and iniquity (Psalms 32:5; 38:18).

The Greek word for "confess" is *homologeo*. This is a compound word consisting of two words *homo* and *logeo*. *Homo* means "the same" and *logeo* means "to speak." Together the word means "to speak the same thing." When we say we are confessing, it literally means we are saying the same thing. Confession is the process of coming into agreement with the Lord and saying the same thing that He says.

Most of the time the New Testament writers use the word confess primarily as a declaration or profession. They encourage us to confess Jesus before men (Matt. 10:32), confess Jesus as Lord (Rom. 10:9), confess the Son (1 John 2:23), and confess that Jesus Christ came in the flesh (1 John 4:2). It may come as a surprise that there are very few instances in the New Testament that mention the confessing of sins. Two of these are in the gospels and two are in the epistles.

Matthew and Mark both tell us that Jews came to John the Baptist at the Jordan river to be baptized by him "as they confessed their sins" (Matt. 3:5; Mark 1:5). This confession of sins that the Jews did was not related to salvation and their acceptance of what Jesus had done for them on the cross. This was several years before the cross. It obviously did not relate to that. We would be mistaken to say that the Jews confessing their sins at the Jordan is a prescriptive model for Christians. Confession of sins for the Jews was more linked to a traditional, ceremonial process that all Jews would have been familiar with at that time.

The epistles of the New Testament have served as the source of instruction and practice for Christians for the last 2000 years. There are six writers who penned the twenty-one epistles to the churches. In them, Paul, Peter, Jude, and the writer of Hebrews never mentioned confessing sins. John and James both mentioned confessing sins once (1 John 1:9 and James 5:16).

James 5:16 is very clear. It says, "confess your sins to one another, and pray for one another so that you may be healed." The most obvious thing we notice in this verse is that we are told to confess our sins *to another person*. This is not a confession of our sins to God. James encouraged us to do this, but it is something that we normally find very uncomfortable to do. It is often difficult to humble ourselves and bring our sin into the light. Nonetheless, it is a good practice, and James told us that if we would confess our sins to one another and pray for each other, we would experience healing.

It is worth noting that James was actually addressing the nature of corporate life within the church. Corporate life refers to how we interact and relate with others in the body of Christ. He asked the question, "What is the source of quarrels and conflicts among you?" (James 4:1). He then went on to speak about several different reasons why there were problems in the church to which he was writing. He specifically pointed out how they were speaking against one another within the church (James 4:11). All this led to his conclusion in chapter five where he encouraged them to confess their sins to one another. Their quarrels and conflicts had caused suffering both spiritually and physically. James was not necessarily talking about personal sins like lying, sexual immorality, and drunkenness. He was most likely talking about sins within the church like division, strife, and jealousy. These are grievous sins to the Lord because God is One (Eph. 4:4-6), and He loves unity. It causes hurt in His body whenever that unity is broken through division and strife (1 Cor. 1:10-13; 3:3; 2 Cor. 12:20). James was helping us to understand that if and when this happens in the church, we should confess it to one another so that we may all be healed and restored to unity with one another.

James was explaining a foundational truth of how we are to relate with one another in the body of Christ. We struggle to understand and practice this type of interaction for a couple of reasons. First, we are very individualistic-minded people. Each of us has a personal relationship with the Lord, but it is always in the context of the body of Christ of which we are only one member of many (1 Cor. 12:12; 14). Our relationship with God is personal, but not private. James was helping us to understand the importance of confession in the context of the corporate body and how it affects each of us individually. This is why in James 5:15-16 he used both singular and plural pronouns in his discussion. Those in the body that were suffering would experience healing as they confessed their sins to one another. The members of the body would forgive anyone who had caused the wrong.

He said,

> Is anyone among you sick? Then he must call for the elders of the church and they are to pray over him, anointing him with oil in the name of the Lord; and the prayer offered in faith will restore the one who is sick, and the Lord will raise him up, and *if he has committed sins, they will be forgiven him* (James 5:14-15).

Notice that James never questioned if this person's sins would be forgiven. He recognized that this would be a normal response from the other members of the body since they already understood they were forgiven by God and that the normal response was to forgive others just as they had been forgiven in Christ (Eph. 4:32; Col. 3:13).

Second, church life in the New Testament looked a lot different than it does today. Church happened in the home and usually in small groups of believers who practiced their faith very intimately with one another. It was not like church today where you come, participate in a worship service, and go home. Often, we have very little substantial interaction with others. It was not this way in the New Testament churches. When there was a problem among the believers, it was felt at a deep level. This is why James was sharing how important it was to walk openly and humbly with one another. The unity and peace in the body was very real and necessary for the body to be healthy. The same remains true today.

This leaves 1 John 1:9 as the only verse in all the epistles that speaks about confessing sins. In this verse John said, "If we confess our sins, He is faithful and righteous to forgive us our sins and to cleanse us from all unrighteousness." This is the go-to verse for anyone who teaches that believers need to confess their sins in order to be forgiven. But is that really what John was teaching? The background and context of John's epistle will help to understand what he meant.

John was writing to a church that was impacted by the early teachings of gnostics. Gnosticism had already become a concern in the early church within just a few years after the life of Christ. Gnosticism ultimately became a very complex system of beliefs that tried to undermine the basic beliefs of Christianity. One aspect of gnosticism specifically is important if we want to understand John's comments in 1 John 1.

Out of their struggle to reconcile the evil they saw in the world, gnostics developed a strange belief that people were divine souls trapped in a natural, physical body. They created a dichotomy between the physical and spiritual realms. They believed that God was not concerned with the physical because it was evil. They concluded that they could do whatever they wanted with their bodies and it did not matter. The only thing that mattered was the divine soul.

This belief led the gnostics to teach that Jesus could not have been a man with a physical body or He would have been evil. They taught that He was only a divine soul and "appeared" to people as an expression of who He was as a spirit. They would use arguments like Jesus walking on water (Matt. 14:22-27; Mark 6:47-52); Jesus escaping masses of people who wanted to throw Him off a cliff (Luke 4:28-30); and Jesus walking through the door in the upper room (John 20:19; 26) as arguments for their belief. You can see how young believers could have been influenced by this type of teaching.

Some of these gnostic teachers had evidently made their way into the church and John addressed this issue in 1 John. He started his first epistle like this:

> What was from the beginning, what we have heard, what we have seen with our eyes, what we have looked at and touched with our hands, concerning the Word of life—and the life was manifested, and we have seen and testify and proclaim to you the eternal life, which was with the Father and was manifested to us—what we have seen and heard we proclaim to you also (1 John 1:1-3a).

We pick up John's tone immediately. He was obviously talking to these false teachers. The first thing he said was that he had actually touched Jesus with his own hands! It was impossible for John to believe Jesus did not have a body. John was the one who was reclining against His chest at the last supper (John 13:23).

John went on to say that what they, the apostles, had seen and heard from the Father they proclaimed to them, the gnostics. He wanted the gnostics to believe the truth so they could also become believers. This was an excellent evangelistic sermon directed at those who were false teachers and who did not believe in the truth about Jesus. This is also why John later said, "By this you know the Spirit of God: every spirit that confesses that Jesus Christ has come in the flesh is from God" (1 John 4:2).

John told them that this message was what he and his co-workers heard from God, and it was what they announced to them. He wanted these non-Christian false teachers to understand how to walk in the truth and to receive forgiveness. It is in this context that he told the false teachers what they should do.

They simply needed to do what every unbeliever must do to receive forgiveness. They needed to believe, confess their sins, and personally receive forgiveness. God would obviously be faithful to forgive them of *all* unrighteousness because of His covenant to do so based on the shed blood of Jesus. This is exactly what we should expect based on what we have already seen in the previous chapter on forgiveness. God is not going to withhold His forgiveness from anyone who believes and confesses the truth. This is something that must happen in anyone's life if they are to personally receive forgiveness of their sins. This is what happens for every person at their salvation experience. Each person individually comes to the realization that they have sin in their life and "speak the same thing." This is what it means to confess. When they do this, God is faithful to forgive them. There is nothing in this passage to suggest that confession is something that happens over and over again in the believer's life. In fact, there is no other Scripture written to believers anywhere in the Bible that suggests this in any way. It was simply a foreign concept to the apostles who wrote the New Testament epistles.

If you keep reading 1 John, you will notice that John shifts his attention to believers in the church in chapter two. In 1 John 2:1-2 he said,

> My little children, I am writing these things to you so that you may not sin. And if anyone sins, we have an Advocate with the Father, Jesus Christ the righteous; and He Himself is the propitiation for our sins; and not for ours only, but also for those of the whole world.

Notice how John referred to them as his little children. This was common language for those who were of the faith. Also, notice what John told them if they did sin. He said, "if anyone sins" they have an Advocate, Jesus Christ, who is the propitiation for our sins. This word propitiation means that Jesus has already taken the punishment and paid the price for our forgiveness. And John said He has done this not only for our sins but also for those of the whole world! Notice that John did not tell his little children to confess their sin so they could be forgiven. This would not have been in keeping with the apostle's understanding of forgiveness and confession.

What does all this mean practically in our lives? There are several implications when we begin to understand the truth about confession. I believe a word of reminder is in order at this point. Remember this entire book is about the Christian life. Everything that I am sharing is for believers so they can experience all God has for them as His children. As was the case in the previous chapter on forgiveness, I want to consider a few things about confession that will help us understand it practically. Notice that all three of these statements apply to the life of a Christian.

1. Christians do not have to confess their sins in order to be forgiven.

2. There is not a cause and effect relationship between confession and forgiveness in the life of a Christian.

3. Believing that confession is necessary to be forgiven will lead to fear and doubt in the life of a Christian.

Let's look at each of these statements in detail.

1. Christians do not have to confess their sins in order to be forgiven.

This is a bold thing to say in light of a lot of traditional church teaching. But before you pass judgment on it, let's consider what we have learned so far (here and in Chapter 6 on Forgiveness). According to the Scriptures, anyone who wants to become a Christian must only believe—have faith and truth—in the finished work of Jesus Christ. By finished work, I mean His death on the cross, His burial, and His resurrection from the dead (1 Cor. 15:3-5). Part of that process includes each person coming into agreement with God that they have sinned and need His forgiveness. Remember that confession means "to say the same thing." A person simply says what God already knows about them. When this happens, He is faithful to forgive them. He is faithful to do this because His forgiveness is based on what Jesus did on the cross. His forgiveness is not based on anything else. This person now enters into a relationship with God and becomes His child. They personally and practically receive forgiveness for all of their sins.

If you have done what I have described, then your faith has brought you into a personal relationship with God through Jesus Christ. Living as a Christian for the rest of your life you enjoy the fact that you are completely forgiven. Even if or when you do sin, you know that God has already forgiven you. You also know that He does not remember your sins anymore (Heb. 10:17). This is why you are not taught anywhere in the Scriptures to confess your sins once you are a Christian. You simply move on from your failures with full assurance in your heart knowing that you don't have to focus on your sin anymore.

2. *There is not a cause and effect relationship between confession and forgiveness in the life of a Christian.*

If you believe it is a requirement for you to confess your sins in order to be forgiven after becoming a Christian, you haven't fully understood God's forgiveness. God's forgiveness is complete. Jesus died for all sins for all time, and when He did, God forgave all sins for all time (remember the diagram in Chapter 6). God doesn't have an issue with sins anymore. The problem comes when you don't believe this truth and make your sins an issue between you and God. What do you think is God's response to you when you confess your sins and ask for forgiveness? I believe His answer is "I have already done that!"

Let me clarify what I am saying. I am *not* saying that you cannot confess your sins to God. I *am* saying that you should not believe you *have* to confess your sins in order to be forgiven. I want to go on record as saying, if you want to continue to confess your sins, that's fine. I do encourage you to not believe that you must confess your sins in order to experience God's forgiveness. There is not a cause and effect relationship between confession and forgiveness in your life. His forgiveness is a gift that He gave you when you first believed. From that day on you simply enjoy the reality that you are forgiven. There is no condition on God's forgiveness for you as His child. There is nothing you can do to earn it. This is the good news of the gospel!

3. Believing that confession is necessary to be forgiven will lead to fear and doubt in the life of a believer.

How can you ever have confidence and full assurance that you are totally forgiven if your forgiveness depends on your confession? What if you miss a sin or forget about one? Do you have to name each sin that you commit in order to know God has forgiven you for all of them? Do you just say a "blanket" confession prayer to cover any possible sins you may have committed each day? Or can you do that every week? Do you see where all these questions are leading? It actually begins to sound absurd. This is not what the Christian life looks like, and it is not how God wants you to live. That is why the writers of the New Testament don't tell Christians to confess their sins. You don't have to focus on sin and confess over and over again as part of your daily routine. The apostles understood the power of the finished work of Jesus, and they knew that it was enough for your forgiveness, once and for all.

Being free from the burden of confession changes the way you relate to God. God is not sitting in heaven with a tally board making sure you have confessed all your sins to Him. He settled the issue of you receiving His forgiveness at the cross. Don't let confession become another requirement in your relationship with God. Receive the truth, "draw near with a sincere heart in full assurance of faith," and "hold fast the confession of your hope without wavering" (Heb. 10:22-23).

🧠 *Encountering the Truth*

Truth: Confessing your sins is a vital part of your salvation experience, but after you receive forgiveness for all of your sins and become a Christian, confession is not necessary to receive God's forgiveness.

Faith Declaration: As a child of God, I do not have to confess my sins in order to be forgiven. I am already forgiven as an unconditional expression of God's love for me that He demonstrated at the cross when Jesus shed His blood.

🚶 *Walking in the Truth*

Continue to renew your mind in the truth that as a believer you are already completely forgiven by God. Recognize that confession is not a requirement that God puts on you in order to enjoy His forgiveness. If you do sin, hold on to this truth and look to Jesus, who is your advocate with the Father. Believe that God will always and forever honor His covenant with His Son on your behalf. You are free from fear, guilt, and condemnation, and you don't need to continually rehearse your wrongs before God.

8

SIN

"And if you do not do well, sin is crouching at the door; and its desire is for you, but you must master it."

~ *Genesis 4:7b*

What shall we say then? Are we to continue in sin so that grace may increase? May it never be! How shall we who died to sin still live in it?

~ *Romans 6:1-2*

One of the most comforting truths that I have come to know and believe is that God has provided everything that we need to live the Christian life. He doesn't leave us to live parts of our Christian life in our own strength or effort, only to struggle with failure and frustration. The great news is that "His divine power has granted to us everything pertaining to life and godliness" (2 Peter 1:3). This means that everything we need to live in fullness as believers has already been provided for us through a true knowledge of Him who has called us. This is the goal of this book—discovering the true knowledge of Jesus and then walking in the reality of that knowledge in our lives. As we do this, we experience a deeper measure of freedom in life and a security in our relationship with God that He desired from the very beginning of time. He did not create us to be religious but to be in relationship.

At some time during our lives we all struggle with sin. It's obviously not the most popular topic of conversation. But like the elephant in the room, we just need to acknowledge it and talk about it. Maybe you find yourself stuck in some area of sin, and you are searching for the "breakthrough" your heart desires (see Romans 7:21-25). It might be a sin pattern that has taken a stronghold in your life and has become that "sin which so easily entangles us" (Heb. 12:1). Sometimes it can be pride, selfishness, or any thoughts or attitudes that are sinful. If this sounds familiar to you, then I am getting ready to share some of the best news you will ever hear!

What would you say if I were to ask you, "What is the difference between sin and sins?" At first glance you might say that one is singular and the other is plural. That is the response I get from most people when I ask them this question. The truth is that there is a huge difference between sin and sins, and seeing the difference is the first key to learning how you can experience complete and full freedom from sin in your life.

We have already seen that through the finished work of Jesus on the cross we received total forgiveness for all our sins—past, present, and future. This means that every sinful act that we have ever done or ever will do is already forgiven. Jesus died for the forgiveness of "sins." These "sins" are all the things that we do in this life that are displeasing to the Lord, done out of the flesh, apart from faith, and contrary to the character and nature of God. However, "sin" is altogether another thing.

The story of Cain and Abel helps us see the difference between sin and sins. The story is very familiar. Cain and Abel both brought a sacrifice to God. Cain brought a sacrifice from the fruit of the ground and Abel from the firstlings of his flock. God had regard for Abel's sacrifice and rejected Cain's sacrifice. Cain had a very normal response. He got his feelings hurt, copped an attitude, and became "very angry and his countenance fell" (Gen. 4:5).

> Then the Lord said to Cain, "Why are you angry? And why has your countenance fallen? If you do well, will not your countenance be lifted up? And if you do not do well, sin is crouching at the door; and its desire is for you, but you must master it" (Gen. 4:6-7).

This is the first reference to sin in the Bible. God told Cain that sin was crouching at his door and that its desire was for him. This is a classic use of personification where the writer gives Sin an actual personality as if it is some type of living entity. (I will capitalize Sin in the remainder of the book to help distinguish it as a unique entity separate from sins that we commit.) God then told Cain that if he did well he could overcome, but if he did not do well, Sin was waiting to pounce upon him because its desire was for him. Cain must master it.

It is very clear from this passage that Sin was something outside of Cain and something that had its own desire. It was something that Cain must attempt to master. In this story, Sin took advantage through Cain's anger to stir up within him the desire to kill his brother. And we know the rest of this tragic story. Sin in fact had its way with Cain and caused him to murder Abel. Murder then became one of Cain's sins that he committed in his life, while Sin was the actual thing that influenced him to do it. Many of us have heard someone say, "The devil made me do it." Actually, it was Sin that made them do it, and Sin is not the devil. Sin is an active and real power at work in the world to cause us to commit sinful acts.

At this point in our conversation we need to take a look back and remember what we have said so far. God chose to forgive all sins for all time through the sacrifice of His Son, Jesus (remember Chapter 6). This means that all the sins that we commit in our lifetime are already forgiven. But this does not mean that God has taken Sin out of the picture. In fact, Sin is just as active now as it was in the days of Cain and Abel. Sin uses any and every tool available to try to cause people to commit sins.

Earlier I mentioned that God has already provided everything we need to live life abundantly in Him. His provision includes everything we need to overcome Sin in our lives. As we correctly understand what this means, we can walk in the truth and be set free.

The mistake that so many of us make is thinking that our problem is the sinful acts that we commit as Christians. We focus on the things we do that we know to be sinful and try to overcome those things through what I call sin management. We try many strategies like self-discipline, accountability with others, or even fasting and praying in order to try to stop committing sins. I truly believe that if we will be completely honest with ourselves, we will all admit we have tried sin management and that it does not work. We inevitably end up doing the same thing again. This leads to frustration and discouragement and ultimately can even cause us to question our relationship with God. The reason for this is because we are not looking at Sin from the proper perspective (remember the importance of perspective in Chapter 2).

We must always remember that our personal sins are not the issue. God has dealt with those by doing what only He can do. He forgave them—totally and unconditionally. However, there is still the issue of Sin that we must address. This is where we find God's perfect remedy. God knew in His infinite wisdom that, just like Cain, we too would be unable to master Sin. He knew that if we were faced with the power of Sin, we would always lose and end up committing sins. Even so, in His great love for us, He forgave all our sins and His forgiveness will always cover any sin we ever commit. This is an immeasurable gift of God's grace!

Does this amazing truth of God's unconditional forgiveness mean that we are to continue sinning so that God's grace and forgiveness can just increase more? Paul asked this very question in Romans. He said,

> What shall we say then? Are we to continue in
> sin so that grace may increase? May it never be!
> How shall we who died to sin still live in it? Or
> do you not know that all of us who have been

> baptized into Christ Jesus have been baptized
> into His death? (Rom. 6:1-3).

These verses contain one of the most powerful truths that we can ever know as Christians. It shifts the entire focus away from the issue of sins onto God's perfect remedy against the power of Sin.

God did the unthinkable. He caused us to be in Christ while He was dying on the cross so that we would die with Him. While Jesus was dying on the cross for our redemption, the forgiveness of our sins, we were also dying with Him so that we would die to the power of Sin. This means that instead of God taking the power of Sin out of the world, he killed us instead! We are dead to Sin, and Sin no longer has power over us.

Just think about this. Now we are in a totally new position with respect to Sin. When Sin comes to us with its diabolical plan to cause us to commit sins, we are dead to it! Paul told us simply and succinctly that "he who has died is freed from sin" (Rom. 6:7). This means that we actually don't have the strength in ourselves to stop doing the specific sins that cause us to stumble. Our ultimate victory is in the reality that God has provided a perfect remedy for us in Christ. The only way we can stop committing sins is to be free from the power of Sin, and this is exactly what Christ has done for us. We cannot overcome Sin in our own strength. Sin will always win. This is why our old man (*anthrópos*, remember Chapter 2) "was crucified with Him, in order that our body of sin might be done away with, so that we would no longer be slaves to sin" (Rom. 6:6). The truth is that we have been ultimately freed through our death with Christ, so that "we too might walk in newness of life" (Rom. 6:4).

This new life is one characterized by the awareness and reality of who we are as the new man in Christ Jesus. We are no longer weak and helpless against the power of Sin, but we are now alive together with Christ. Sin has no power over us. We overcome by abiding in the reality of who we are based on all that God has done for us. Living any other way, we are doomed for failure and a life defined by discouragement and despair.

Our focus now is on the life that we have in Christ. He is our life and because we are trusting in His life within us we no longer focus on Sin or sins.

Forgiveness has removed our sins and our death with Christ has set us free from the power of Sin.

God has perfectly provided everything we need. In the same way that God forgave all sins once and for all when Jesus died, in His death, Jesus also "died to sin once and for all; but the life that He lives, He lives to God" (Rom. 6:10). This means that His and our death to Sin is final and complete. Now Jesus lives His life for the glory of God, and He is doing this in and through us. Thanks be to God through Jesus Christ our Lord!

One thing I do not ever want to do is share an essential truth and leave someone asking, "What does that mean for my life?" or "How does it work practically for me?" We must be able to bring the truth to the most practical areas of our lives.

This does not always mean that the practical application of truth in your life will seem easy or even natural at times. In fact, the application of truth in your life often comes with a very real sense of discomfort. This happens when you have become more comfortable with something less than the truth in your life for a long time. So much so, that the full truth can almost appear as a lie when you first encounter it. But if you will exercise your faith and trust what God is showing you to be true, He is faithful to establish the truth in your heart and mind. It is the Spirit's job to lead you into all the truth (John 16:13). You will ultimately be transformed by the truth and the truth will make you free. This is practical Christianity and it is spiritual and very real.

When I first became a Christian in 1986, I was twenty-one years old. I had a lot of areas in my life that were unhealthy. Because of many choices that I had made during my adult years between the age of fifteen and twenty-one, I had developed many sinful habits. It was very natural for me to be involved in these activities, and I never really gave it a second thought. One day the Holy Spirit began to convict me of my sin and ultimately led me to the revelation of Jesus and my need to believe in Him. When I received the truth and confessed my sins, God was truly faithful and righteous to forgive me completely (1 John 1:9). However, there was one important thing I did not know at that point. I had no idea that I had died with Christ and was dead to the power of Sin in my life. No one told me that I had become a new creation and was alive to God in Christ Jesus (Rom. 6:10-11).

After this initial experience of becoming a Christian, I became aware that I still had areas of sinful behavior in my life. As a believer, I obviously knew that these habits were wrong, unhealthy, and unwanted. There was one big problem. I did not know how to get out of these sinful patterns. Like many of you, I began my journey of trying to live free from my destructive behaviors. I tried a number of sin management tools. I got involved in accountability groups with other men. They would ask me the "hard questions" regularly and I would try to answer honestly. Sometimes I would be honest and confess that I had failed, and they would pray for me and encourage me to try harder. Other times I would just lie to them and say I was doing well when in reality I was failing miserably in some area of my life.

This is the place that many Christians find themselves. They are stuck in the in-between land. Because they do not know the truth, they are living powerless to overcome Sin in their lives. They know that they are saved and forgiven—though sometimes they are not always very confident—but they have not come to a full awareness of who they are in Christ as a new creation, dead to the power of Sin, and alive to God in Christ Jesus. They are stuck. Some spend long periods of time in this place, discouraged and defeated, until they find the truth that I am explaining in this chapter.

In my case, I was never able to "get the victory" in certain areas of my life. I found this to be very discouraging. And then the Lord began to reveal this wonderful truth to me. I began to see, in the Scriptures and through a process of many different events, the truth that my old man had actually died with Christ. Because of this death, I had been set free from the power of Sin. I began to realize that it was not my behavior that I needed to change, but my understanding of my relationship to the power of Sin. I realized that Sin no longer had any power over me to cause me to commit sins. I had a new reality from which I could live and I began to choose that reality. I began to transform my mind with this life-changing truth (Rom. 12:2). I learned to trust the Lord to make this truth real in my life. And as I did this God was faithful to bring me to the place where I began to experience this truth as a reality in my life.

As a natural byproduct of this truth becoming manifested in my life, I no longer struggled with the old sin patterns. I began to practically experience the power of Christ's life in me that was much greater than the power of Sin. I came to understand that the "law of the Spirit of life in Christ Jesus had set me free from the law of sin and of death" (Rom. 8:2). The revelation of this truth changed my life. It brought me into the victory that my heart so desired. It gave me a much deeper appreciation for what God had done for me in Christ. It caused me to see and believe that all of God's children can walk in freedom from the power of Sin. Not because of their own strength to do what is right, but because of the life of Jesus living inside of them.

Encountering the Truth

Truth: Your old self was crucified with Christ. Through your death with Him, you have been set free from the power of Sin because he who has died is freed from Sin.

Faith Declaration: I am dead to Sin, but alive to God in Christ Jesus.

Walking in the Truth

Choose each day to believe that you are free from the power of Sin in your life and alive to God in Christ Jesus. If you are battling with sins in your life, do not focus on those sins. Instead, focus your faith and attention on the truth that you are completely forgiven and you are dead to the power of Sin in your life today. Trust the life of Jesus Christ in you to set you free from the power of Sin. Continue to walk in the truth in this way until you are transformed and living free from Sin.

9

FLESH

"It is the Spirit who gives life; the flesh profits nothing; the words that I have spoken to you are spirit and are life."

~ *John 6:63*

But I say, walk by the Spirit, and you will not carry out the desire of the flesh. For the flesh sets its desire against the Spirit, and the Spirit against the flesh; for these are in opposition to one another, so that you may not do the things that you please.

~ *Galatians 5:16-17*

A common question I hear from people is "If everything you say about the new creation in Christ, forgiveness, grace, and our freedom from Sin is true, why do Christians still commit sins?" It is a good question and one that deserves a good answer. If, in fact, God has forgiven all our sins, our old man has died with Christ, and we have been raised in newness of life so that Sin has no power over us, why do we still sin?

The answer to this question will provide another essential truth that is necessary for us to live in the fullness of our divine life as God's children. A correct understanding of what the Bible means by "flesh" is at the center of the answer to this question.

The flesh has been a topic of biblical scholars for centuries. Without going into too much background, it seems that the idea of flesh was already present in pre-Christian literature, so when Jesus and the apostles used the word it was not a totally foreign concept. However, it does seem that the idea of "flesh" was more developed in Paul's thought. He gives it much more meaning and uses it to explain a very important aspect of the believer's life. But before we look at that, let's do a little background work to develop a basic understanding of what we mean by "flesh."

The first and most obvious meaning of "flesh" is anything pertaining to the "skin and bone" aspect of life. This may refer to the flesh or meat of an animal or even our own flesh and bone. The Bible uses the term in this way when it refers to the flesh of the sacrifices that were offered to God by the priest under the Old Covenant (Lev. 4:11). In the same way, John saw an angel standing and calling to the birds of the air to come and "eat the flesh of kings and the flesh of commanders and the flesh of mighty men and the flesh of horses and of those who sit on them and the flesh of all men" (Rev. 19:18).

"Flesh" can also be a reference to all of mankind. Luke tells us, "All flesh will see the salvation of God" (Luke 3:6), and when Jesus was praying to the Father, He recognized that He had been given "authority over all flesh" (John 17:2). Both of these meanings are quite literal and easy to understand.

There is another dimension to the meaning of "flesh" that is less concrete and more difficult to understand. It is this use of the term that applies to us as believers.

Jesus used the word "flesh" in a couple of different ways. He spoke about the marriage relationship between man and woman and said, "... the two shall become one flesh" (Matt. 19:5). This is obviously a reference to the physical union between man and woman achieved through sexual relations. However, it also speaks of a deeper union whereby the man and woman achieve a level of intimacy through relational interaction and selfless sacrifice in the context of their marriage. You see this often when you are around two people who have been married for many years. It is as though they are always "on the same page" in the way they think and express themselves. This is a deep unity that God intends for man and woman to enjoy in the context of the marriage relationship.

Jesus also used "flesh" in reference to His own life when He spoke about His flesh being the bread which He gives for the life of the world (John 6:51). He told us, "He who eats My flesh and drinks My blood abides in Me, and I in him" (John 6:56). There is another way that Jesus used "flesh" and this is the one that is most important for us to understand.

When Jesus asked His disciples who people were saying He was, Peter answered and said, "You are the Christ, the Son of the living God" (Matt. 16:16). Jesus responded to Peter with a wholehearted affirmation and declared that Peter was blessed because "flesh and blood" had not revealed this truth to him (Matt. 16:17). He had received the revelation from God concerning who Jesus was and this was from a source that was outside of his own natural ability through reasoning. John used the idea of "flesh" in the same way when he told us that children of God are born "not of blood nor of the will of the flesh nor of the will of man, but of God" (John 1:13).

Jesus also said, "It is the Spirit who gives life; the flesh profits nothing; the words that I have spoken to you are spirit and are life" (John 6:63). He was telling us that only the Spirit can give life and our own natural ability and understanding profit nothing in our quest to know and understand who God is. From these passages we see that "flesh" is something directly related to our *natural ability* that is distinctly different from God's power and ability.

Paul picked up where Jesus left off and developed this idea of "flesh" extensively. Paul used the word "flesh" (the Greek word *sarx*) over 90 times in his letters. It was obviously a very important concept for him. He used the term in the same way as Jesus and John, but in a more expansive manner to describe the natural condition of the human race. This condition is not confined to non-believers. He told the believers in Corinth that he could not speak to them as spiritual men, "but as to men of flesh, as to infants in Christ" (1 Cor. 3:1) who were still "fleshly" (1 Cor. 3:3). From these statements we see it is possible to be a believer and to still deal with some aspect of the "flesh."

We can use Paul's many different uses of the word to form a working definition of "flesh," but no one can say with total confidence exactly what is meant by this term. Here is one man's description of "flesh" that I believe highlights many of the different nuances of this important word.

> Flesh is a condition in which man operates out of his own resources, doing things his own way. Flesh is the self-centered source upon which we depend to get our needs met. Some describe it as a tool box with which each person attempts to deal with life or fix his problems. Others describe flesh as habit patterns, the way in which man attempts to cope with life in his own strength (Jack Cole, from an unpublished teaching titled "The Flesh").

Unlike some, I do not believe that "flesh" is referring to our sinful nature or our old man. "Flesh" cannot be referring to the sinful nature or the old man because we have already seen clearly (remember Chapters 2 and 8) that God has dealt a final death blow to our sinful nature on the cross so that we are now a new creation which has been created in "righteousness and holiness of the truth" (Eph. 4:24). Since this is true, "flesh" must be some other part of us that can remain present and active in our lives after we become a new creation in Christ.

Only on two occasions do the New Testament writers refer to our former life before Christ as being in the flesh (Rom. 7:5; Eph. 2:3). All the other references to "flesh" are made in the context of believers. This tells us that "flesh" is a very real aspect of the Christian life and one we need to understand properly.

If we work from the definition that I offered above, it makes sense that "flesh" is a condition that we can choose to walk in at any given time in our Christian journey. This simply means that, at the times of our own choosing or because of habit patterns, we can act according to the flesh. When we do this, we choose independence and self-sufficiency. We step out of dependence on the life of Christ within us and walk in our own strength and use our own resources to deal with life's situations and circumstances. We refuse to walk in the Spirit, and we walk according to the flesh. Paul explained this in Romans 8. He said,

> For those who are according to the flesh set their minds on the things of the flesh, but those who are according to the Spirit, the things of the Spirit. For the mind set on the flesh is death, but the mind set on the Spirit is life and peace, because the mind set on the flesh is hostile toward God; for it does not subject itself to the law of God, for it is not even able to do so, and those who are in the flesh cannot please God (Rom. 8:5-8).

The first thing to note about this passage is that it comes right in the middle of an entire chapter that is devoted specifically to the life of the believer. Romans 8 begins with, "Therefore there is now no condemnation for *those who are in Christ Jesus*" (Rom. 8:1). The rest of the chapter is describing the life of those who are in Christ. It would be a bit misleading to say that verses 5-8 are contrasting an unbeliever and believer. Instead, it is better to say that these verses are contrasting the possible condition of a believer at any given time. Paul was simply saying that it is totally possible for a believer to either "set their mind on the things of the flesh" or to set their mind on the "things of the Spirit."

This is the real conflict and challenge for the believer at any given time. But Paul makes it clear that "we are under obligation, not to the flesh, to live according to the flesh" (Rom. 8:12).

There is another passage of Scripture that takes this idea further. In Galatians 5, Paul said,

> But I say, walk by the Spirit, and you will not carry out the desire of the flesh. For the flesh sets its desire against the Spirit, and the Spirit against the flesh; for these are in opposition to one another, so that you may not do the things that you please (Gal. 5:16-17).

These verses tell us that there is a real battle in the life of the believer between the Spirit and the flesh. These two are setting their desire against one another. Unfortunately, because of a misunderstanding of "flesh," many Christians miss this battle and involve themselves in some other type of struggle that is misguided. Instead of focusing their attention on life in the Spirit as the ultimate means to win the battle they are experiencing within themselves, they do all sorts of interesting things. They pray for deliverance from certain areas of their lives or do spiritual warfare, thinking that it is the devil's fault for their struggle. This may very well be the case in some instances. However, I have found that it is not the root of the problem for many believers. The problem is the flesh. And the only solution for the flesh is the Spirit!

If we walk by the Spirit, we will not carry out the desire of the flesh. This means that there are desires inside of us that come from ourselves. It is our natural condition that remains as long as we are in this life. This is why Paul said, "... the life which I now live in the *flesh* I live by faith in the Son of God" (Gal. 2:20). He understood that while he continued to live in the natural condition, he still had to make the choice to depend on the indwelling Spirit of Christ to lead, direct, and animate his very being. When we fail to do this, the desire of our flesh motivates us to act out independently of the Lord.

We see from this passage in Galatians 5 that the deeds of the flesh are evident and obvious. These are:

> ...immorality, impurity, sensuality, idolatry, sorcery, enmities, strife, jealousy, outbursts of anger, disputes, dissensions, factions, envying, drunkenness, carousing and things like these (Gal. 5:19-21).

This is quite an unattractive list. However, it is possible that you are capable of these types of behaviors if you do not walk by the Spirit. Paul said specifically that "you may not do the things that you please" (Gal. 5:17). It is still possible to sin because of the desire of the flesh that sets itself against the Spirit in your life. However, the good news of the truth is that if you will simply choose the Spirit in your life then you will not fulfill the desire of the flesh in any way.

Paul finished this important passage by telling us "those who belong to Christ Jesus have crucified the flesh with its passions and desires" (Gal. 5:24). This process of crucifying the flesh takes place as you walk by the Spirit. This is why he finished the entire discussion by saying:

> If we live by the Spirit, let us also walk by the Spirit. Let us not become boastful, challenging one another, envying one another (Gal. 5:25-26).

Do you see the attitude that you choose to have in this entire process? You learn to completely rely on the life of the Spirit within you in total humility and dependence. There is no room for pride and arrogance in this process because all of us are susceptible to the desire of the flesh having its way in our lives.

The best news of all is that we are righteous in Christ Jesus and do not have the natural inclination towards the flesh any longer. We have the desire within us to be righteous because that is what is natural for Jesus. When and if we do succumb to the flesh, we know that we are not condemned to live by it. We simply thank God for the forgiveness that is already there. We refocus our faith on the Spirit within and recognize that God has provided everything we need in Christ Jesus!

There is another element of the flesh to discuss if we are to fully understand this important truth. Paul said, we are those "who worship in the Spirit of God and glory in Christ Jesus and put no confidence in the flesh" (Phil. 3:3). He went on to say that he had every reason to put his confidence in the flesh. He carefully highlighted all the reasons that he could have put confidence in his flesh. He was

> ...circumcised the eighth day, of the nation of Israel, of the tribe of Benjamin, a Hebrew of Hebrews; as to the Law, a Pharisee; as to zeal, a persecutor of the church; as to the righteousness which is in the Law, found blameless (Phil. 3:5-6).

This is a pretty impressive list of personal pedigree and accomplishments. Paul covered the gamut. He mentioned his ancestral heritage, nationality, family connections, religious accomplishments, devotional service to God, and personal piety. I am not sure there could be a guy who was more connected and more accomplished than Paul. Yet he said that he could not put his confidence in these things. Paul recognized that in the natural realm all these were things he considered important and an actual means of gain. His background, training, and reputation were things that would gain him acceptance, high status, and prestige to open doors of opportunity for him. Despite all of this, Paul said he was willing to "count all things to be loss in view of the surpassing value of knowing Christ Jesus my Lord" (Phil. 3:8).

This opens up a huge truth about the flesh that moves you into a deeper understanding of your identity in the Lord. You must be willing to give up all the things in your life that you see as strengths and a means of gain. Attaching false security or finding your identity in these things can actually keep you from knowing the Lord Jesus more intimately. Jesus wants to be your source of strength and will not compete with the natural strengths of your flesh.

This may sound like a difficult word and I admit it is challenging, but I can assure you it is life-giving. The Lord knows how prone we are to put our confidence in things that are not capable of sustaining and fulfilling us. He will work to root these things out of our hearts. When we refuse to put our confidence in the flesh, we will have a greater intimate knowledge of Jesus. This is one of the most significant revelations I have ever had apart from my salvation. This truth has the power to set us free in a deep and profound way. (I will discuss this more in Chapter 11 on Suffering.)

The world around us constantly lures us to celebrate our strengths and to identify ourselves with so many things other than Jesus. It is very easy to fall into this destructive trap. But when we see the deceptiveness of our flesh, we can be set free and find our life and identity fully and completely in Christ.

Your greatest reward in this life is to gain Christ. It is not to gain the accolades, respect, and honor of people. As you live for His glory and not your own, your heart will long for only one thing. You will desire to gain Christ and to be found in Him (Phil. 3:9). This is a life-long process and one that will always be calling you on "toward the goal for the prize of the upward call of God in Christ Jesus" (Phil. 3:14).

The flesh is a very practical reality for believers. You need to understand how it operates in your life. It is not something you need to worry about or be obsessed with, but something that you know you can be free from as you walk in the Spirit through the power of the life of Christ in you. Like Paul, you too can proclaim with confidence, "Wretched man that I am! Who will set me free from the body of this death? Thanks be to God through Jesus Christ our Lord!" (Rom. 7:24-25).

Encountering the Truth

Truth: The flesh is a normal experience for everyone. You are not meant to live your life according to the flesh, but by the Spirit of Christ who lives in you.

Faith Declaration: I am not under obligation to the flesh, to do the things of the flesh, but I live by the Spirit through which I crucify the flesh daily. Jesus lives in me, through me, as me.

Walking in the Truth

Each day you have the ability to recognize when you are acting according to the flesh and choose to walk by the

Spirit. You can bring those natural inclinations, desires, and impulses to the cross and put them to death by an act of your faith and will. This process will become easier as you recognize that the deeds of the flesh only bring destruction in your life and in the lives of others around you, and the activity of the Spirit brings life! As you live by the Spirit you will not fulfill the desire of the flesh.

10

SPIRIT

However, you are not in the flesh but in the Spirit, if indeed the Spirit of God dwells in you.
~ *Romans 8:9a*

Because you are sons, God has sent forth the Spirit of His Son into our hearts, crying, "Abba! Father!"
~ *Galatians 4:6*

After more than three decades of being a believer, one of the most controversial topics I have seen among Christians is the topic of the Spirit. I have often asked myself, "Why is it that one of the most core aspects of Christianity is surrounded by so much controversy that tends to divide fellow Christians from one another?" I think the only real answer to that question is in the truth that the devil hates God and wants to undermine who He is in any way he can.

The Spirit is fully God and the vital connection between God and man. The role and activity of the Spirit in the world and in the life of the believer is foundational to God's plan.

All of us have been impacted in some way by various views and teachings about the Spirit. Some of us come from more conservative and reformed backgrounds where we learned that the role of the Spirit is not a very active part of the believer's daily experience. Others of us come from a more Pentecostal or Charismatic background where we were taught the Spirit is a very active part of the believer's life.

I met the Lord and was discipled in a Baptist church and eventually earned my PhD from a Baptist seminary. I am grateful for my Baptist roots. I learned to love the Scriptures and to have a heart for missions and the nations. But I remember vividly in those days of my spiritual formation I was taught to be careful how friendly I was with the Holy Spirit. Don't get me wrong, the people who impacted my life believed the Spirit played a role in our salvation, but past that things became a bit fuzzy, and they didn't see things the same as our more charismatic and pentecostal friends.

I learned quickly that much of the controversy arises when believers begin to speak about the gifts or manifestations of the Spirit as well as the baptism of the Spirit. I will say right up front, I will not deal with either one of these topics in detail here. I do not believe that either one of these topics should be the main focus in our understanding of the Spirit, but I do believe we need to understand the function of the Spirit and our relationship with Him in our daily lives.

Jesus gave some of the most clear instruction about the role and activity of the Spirit found anywhere in the Scriptures.

We find much of His teaching about the Spirit in the gospel of John. In John 16 Jesus tells his disciples that it is better for Him to go away so that the Helper could come (John 16:7). He promised to send the Spirit and that He would be active in the lives of believers as well as in the world.

Jesus told us what the role of the Spirit would be in the believer's life. He said,

> "But when He, the Spirit of truth, comes, He will guide you into all the truth; for He will not speak on His own initiative, but whatever He hears, He will speak; and He will disclose to you what is to come. He will glorify Me, for He will take of Mine and will disclose it to you. All things that the Father has are Mine; therefore I said that He takes of Mine and will disclose it to you" (John 16:13-15).

Jesus said the Spirit would guide "you" into all the truth. "You" is directed to the disciples, those who follow Jesus and believe in Him. This is a wonderful promise that Jesus made to all of us who believe in Him. The Spirit will guide us into all the truth. The Spirit glorifies Jesus in our lives and gives us everything that belongs to Him. Wow! I am so thankful that the Spirit is busy in my life leading me into all the truth and giving to me all that belongs to Jesus (1 Cor. 2:12). Aren't you glad that the Spirit is doing this in your life right now?

The greatest truth that the Spirit is leading you into is the fact that you are a child of God. God has sent His Spirit into your heart and He constantly testifies to you that you are a child of God until you finally cry out "Abba! Father!" (Rom. 8:15-17; Gal. 4:6-7). While Jesus was on the earth, He was completely secure in the fact that He was God's Son. The Spirit is giving you that same assurance. He is leading you into full conviction that you have a heavenly Father and you are His child. If you are His child, then you are also an heir of God and fellow heir with Christ (Rom. 8:17). That means everything that belongs to Jesus also belongs to you.

The Spirit is actively involved in God's ultimate purpose of sharing His life with you. The Spirit gives life (John 6:63; 2 Cor. 3:6), and the life that He gives is the life of Jesus. The Spirit of life in Christ Jesus works in your life to continually give you victory over Sin and death (Rom. 8:2). The presence of the Spirit of Christ in you is proof positive that you belong to God (Rom. 8:9), and the Spirit in you "gives life to your mortal body" (Rom. 8:11). When you are being led by the Spirit, you are demonstrating that you are a child of God (Rom. 8:14).

The Spirit bears His fruit of "love, joy, peace, patience, kindness, goodness, faithfulness, gentleness, and self-control" in you (Gal. 5:22). This is the character of Jesus expressing Himself through your life.

The Spirit also helps you when you are weak and don't know how to pray by interceding for you. He knows exactly how to pray because He knows the mind of God and prays according to the will of God (Rom. 8:26-27).

The Spirit baptizes you into the body of Christ when you first believe (1 Cor. 12:13) and then gives you gifts as He wills for the common good of the body of Christ (1 Cor. 12:7; 11). He is a seal and guarantee of your inheritance to come in the future after you die (2 Cor. 1:22; 5:5). Your body is the actual temple of the Spirit and He dwells inside of you (1 Cor. 6:19). These are just a few of the wonderful things the Spirit does in your life as a believer!

In addition to working powerfully in the lives of believers, the Spirit is also active in the world. Jesus said,

> "And He, when He comes, will convict the world concerning sin and righteousness and judgment; concerning sin, because they do not believe in Me; and concerning righteousness, because I go to the Father and you no longer see Me; and concerning judgment, because the ruler of this world has been judged" (John 16:8-11).

These are staple verses for many people who teach about the role of the Spirit in a Christian's life. But I want you to notice an important word in these verses. That word is "world." Jesus said that when the Spirit comes He will convict the world of sin, righteousness, and judgment.

In the Bible, the "world" obviously refers to the physical elements that God has created. But, more importantly, it is a specific reference to unbelievers. God so loved the world He sent His son (John 3:16) so the world might be saved (John 3:17), but the world did not know Him (John 1:10). The god of this world has blinded the minds of the unbelieving (2 Cor. 4:4), and in Christ God was reconciling the world to Himself (2 Cor. 5:19). These verses point clearly to the fact that the "world" refers to unbelievers.

Jesus was telling us that the Spirit will come so that He can bring conviction—understanding and awareness—to the unbelieving world in three areas:

- Sin
- Righteousness
- Judgment

There are two common mistakes that I see people make regarding these verses. First, they miss the fact that the Spirit is convicting the world—unbelievers. Second, they stop reading after verse eight. I pointed out earlier in Chapter 1 in my explanation of Romans 8:28-29 that we need to always keep reading the full context of the Scriptures. If we stop reading at the end of verse eight, we miss the whole point of what Jesus was saying. In John 16:9-11, Jesus explained exactly what He meant by the Spirit convicting the world of sin, righteousness, and judgment.

- Sin ⟶ because they do not believe.

- Righteousness ⟶ because I go to the Father and you no longer see Me.

- Judgment ⟶ because the ruler of this world has been judged.

I love how Jesus was so specific and clear. He didn't leave anything to guesswork. The Spirit's role is to bring conviction to unbelievers in these three areas.

First, the Spirit comes to convict unbelievers that they do not believe. He wants them to see that their unbelief is what is keeping them from God. Jesus said, "This is the work of God, that you believe in Him whom He has sent" (John 6:29), and "He who believes in Him is not judged; he who does not believe has been judged already, because he has not believed in the name of the only begotten Son of God" (John 3:18). Very simply, God wants the world to be saved, and for this to happen they need to believe in Jesus. The Spirit's role is to convict the world of their unbelief so they will come to have faith in Him.

Second, the Spirit convicts the world of righteousness. He does this because Jesus is no longer on the earth as a man for the world to see. Jesus embodied righteousness and demonstrated what it looked like to be and live in right standing with God. But now that He is gone, it is the Spirit's job to show or convict the world what righteousness looks like. This is interesting to think about. The Spirit is showing unbelievers what righteousness looks like since they cannot actually see Jesus. This means that the Spirit is revealing to the world what it means to be in a right relationship with God (remember Chapter 5 on Righteousness). The Spirit is not going around showing the world how wrong they are before God. He is showing them how to be right with God!

Third, the Spirit shows the world that the ruler of this world has already been judged. The ruler of this world is a reference to the devil. Paul called him the "prince of the power of the air" (Eph. 2:2) and the "god of this world" (2 Cor. 4:4). The Spirit's role is to make it evident to the world that the devil has already been judged! The Spirit is revealing to the world before they ever believe that Jesus has already "disarmed the rulers and authorities" and "made a public display of them, having triumphed over them" on the cross (Col. 2:15).

Most of you have probably heard someone say that the role of the Spirit in your life is to convict you of sin. By the time you finish this book, you will see that this doesn't make much sense once you understand what God has done regarding Sin and your sins (remember Chapters 6, 7, and 8). The Scriptures do not teach anywhere that the Spirit convicts believers of their sins.

John 16:8 is the only verse in the Bible that talks about the conviction of sin and this is simply the sin of unbelief. The word "convict" in the Greek means to "show" or "expose." It can also mean to "reprove." The reason why the Spirit does not show or expose our sin—or reprove us about our sin—is because God has forgiven all our sins and they are no longer an issue with the Lord.

If you truly understand who you are in Christ, then you know that you don't need the Spirit to expose your sin. Paul said that the sinful deeds of the flesh are "evident" (Gal. 5:19), and you are to "expose" them yourself (Eph. 5:11). Paul explained in detail how this process works practically in your life. He named a number of sinful activities that should "not even be named among you" (Eph. 5:3). He then said,

> ...you were formerly darkness, but now you are
> Light in the Lord; walk as children of Light (for
> the fruit of the Light consists in all goodness and
> righteousness and truth), trying to learn what is
> pleasing to the Lord (Eph. 5:8-10).

As a believer, you are constantly learning what is pleasing to the Lord and how to walk in the Light. When you do this, "all things become visible when they are *exposed* by the light" (Eph. 5:13). The word "exposed" here is the same word used in other verses for "convict" in different contexts (John 16:8; 1 Cor. 14:24; Jude 1:15). Technically, any "conviction" in our lives comes as the natural result of being in the Light, because Christ has "shone in our hearts" (2 Cor. 4:6), and we are no longer in the darkness. When we "walk in the Light as He Himself is in the Light, we have fellowship with one another, and the blood of Jesus His Son cleanses us from all sin" (1 John 1:7).

Life in the Spirit describes what being a Christian is all about more clearly than any other truth. You were created by God to experience fellowship with Him, and the way this happens is through His Spirit dwelling in you. The Spirit gives life, and His presence in you affirms that you are a child of God and an heir with Christ. Together with the Father and the Son, the Spirit completes and brings to fullness God sharing His life with you.

Encountering the Truth

Truth: The Spirit of Christ, the Holy Spirit, lives inside of you to make known to you and give you everything that belongs to Jesus.

Faith Declaration: The same Spirit that raised Jesus from the dead dwells in my body and He is active in many ways, including testifying that I am a child of God, leading me into all the truth, empowering me to live free from Sin, and manifesting His fruit and gifts in and through my life.

Walking in the Truth

No matter what your views about the Holy Spirit have been in the past, start today to believe that He is living in your body, and that He is the Spirit of Jesus Christ. He has come to live within you to manifest the life of Jesus. Ask the Lord to open your eyes to this reality and to help you to live by the Spirit each and every day.

11

SUFFERING

Suffering is nothing by itself. But suffering shared with the passion of Christ is a wonderful gift, the most beautiful gift, a token of love.

~ Mother Teresa

For to you it has been granted for Christ's sake, not only to believe in Him, but also to suffer for His sake.

~ Philippians 1:29

Nobody wants to hear that suffering is an essential part of being a Christian. I would like to leave this chapter out of the book. But, unfortunately, as much as we don't want to hear it, God has a lot to say about suffering. So, it will serve us well to take a look at this challenging yet important topic. When we understand the truth about suffering, we can accept it as a necessary and beneficial part of living in the ultimate purpose of God.

Life is hard and we don't have the luxury of choosing our experiences. It would be nice if we could take only the good things and leave the bad. But Jesus told us to take heart because in this world we will have tribulation—really hard times—but He has overcome the world (John 16:33). This is a beautiful and encouraging promise, but it presupposes that things will be hard, and none of us like hard.

The good news is that God is faithful through everything we experience and He never wastes anything that happens in our lives. Remember how we saw right in the beginning in Chapter 1 that God works *all things* together for good. "All things" includes the good and the bad. He is using it all to conform us to the image of Christ.

The New Testament is full of references to suffering. The writers use at least five different words that appear over 120 times to describe suffering in one way or another. The most common reference to suffering is the experience of believers who are physically harmed because of their faith in Christ. One of the earliest accounts of this is in Acts when the apostles were flogged for preaching the gospel, and they rejoiced that they were counted worthy to suffer shame for His name (Acts 5:41). They were doing exactly what Jesus had told them to do when He said,

> "Blessed are you when people insult you and persecute you, and falsely say all kinds of evil against you because of Me. Rejoice and be glad, for your reward in heaven is great; for in the

same way they persecuted the prophets who were before you" (Matt. 5:11-12).

The apostles saw suffering as a normal part of the Christian life. Peter told us, "For you have been called for this purpose, since Christ also suffered for you, leaving you an example for you to follow in His steps" (1 Peter 2:21).

When Saul (Paul) was called by the risen Lord on the road to Damascus, he was sent to Ananias. The Lord spoke to Ananias about Saul and said,

> "Go, for he is a chosen instrument of Mine, to bear My name before the Gentiles and kings and the sons of Israel; for I will show him how much he must *suffer* for My name's sake" (Acts 9:15-16).

God had a significant calling for Paul and he was used by God to extend the reach of the gospel more than anyone in the past 2000 years. In addition to proclaiming the name of Jesus, God also spoke about how Paul would suffer as well. All of us would love to hear God speak about how powerfully He is going to use us. But I wonder how we would react if God added that, in addition to being used by Him to do great things, we also "must suffer?"

Paul found out all too well that what God had spoken about him would come to pass. Listen to this extensive description that Paul gave about his suffering:

> Are they servants of Christ?—I speak as if insane—I more so; in far more labors, in far more imprisonments, beaten times without number, often in danger of death. Five times I received from the Jews thirty-nine lashes. Three

> times I was beaten with rods, once I was stoned,
> three times I was shipwrecked, a night and a day
> I have spent in the deep. I have been on frequent
> journeys, in dangers from rivers, dangers from
> robbers, dangers from my countrymen, dangers
> from the Gentiles, dangers in the city, dangers
> in the wilderness, dangers on the sea, dangers
> among false brethren; I have been in labor and
> hardship, through many sleepless nights, in
> hunger and thirst, often without food, in cold
> and exposure. Apart from such external things,
> there is the daily pressure on me of concern for
> all the churches (2 Cor. 11:23-28).

Paul's ministry was marked throughout by suffering, and yet he maintained the most incredible perspective in it all. He said, "For I consider that the sufferings of this present time are not worthy to be compared with the glory that is to be revealed to us" (Rom. 8:18). (We will look at this verse in more detail later in the chapter.)

Most of us will never endure physical harm because of our faith. However, untold numbers of Christians have suffered for their faith over the past 2000 years, and today many of our brothers and sisters in Christ all over the world are undergoing persecution for His name's sake. We should never dismiss the possibility of this happening in our lifetime. The same Peter who told us to follow the example given to us by Christ also told us, "Beloved, do not be surprised at the fiery ordeal among you, which comes upon you for your testing, as though some strange thing were happening to you" (1 Peter 4:12). Peter was encouraging believers who were going through difficult times of persecution to not be surprised as though some "strange thing" was happening to them.

Though we may not experience physical persecution, we will still go through hardship in this life. There are untold trials and adversities that we will experience, and all of those are part of our own suffering.

Next to physical persecution, the most common expression of suffering in the New Testament is that of tribulation and affliction. This can come in all sorts of ways, and none of us are immune from it. This type of suffering comes primarily because of the fallenness of the world. At times the brokenness of the world touches our lives in a personal way and challenges us deeply. It may be something as common as a strained relationship, or it could be something as devastating as an unexpected tragedy that impacts our lives or the life of a loved one. These experiences bring a very real "pressing" in our lives that is painful and at times unbearable. Paul encouraged us in these times to "exult in our tribulations, knowing that tribulation brings about perseverance; and perseverance, proven character; and proven character, hope" (Rom. 5:3-4). We tend to talk a lot about healing and victory and very little about brokenness and weakness. These are a normal part of life, and the truth is that they accomplish something that can only happen when we encounter suffering.

In addition to physical persecution and the pressures of life, we will also experience trials and temptations so that our faith may be refined for the glory of God. I believe that these experiences are also a part of suffering, and we can accept them as transformative tools in our maturing process.

We know that we will encounter "various trials" (James 1:2) and will also be "distressed by various trials" (1 Peter 1:6) for the testing of our faith.

Our faith is so valuable that one day, after it has been tested and refined, it will be the one thing that will bring "glory and honor at the revelation of Jesus Christ" (1 Peter 1:7). It is an incredible thought that when we finally see the Lord face to face, the one thing that will bring Him glory more than anything else is our faith. God is using all our trials to refine our faith and make it more pure than gold.

Once we embrace the role of suffering in our lives, we can even make the choice to suffer the loss of things for the sake of Christ. (I discussed this in Chapter 9 on Flesh.) I know it may be hard to hear, but this is one of the keys to opening a deeper intimacy with Jesus. We need to come to the place where we are willing to count even the good things in our lives as loss for the sake of gaining Christ (Phil. 3:7-8). There is nothing that we possess in our lives that can be compared to the "surpassing value of knowing Christ Jesus" and being "found in Him" (Phil. 3:8). This is only possible as we make the intentional decision to let go of things in which we find identity, strength, and comfort.

I can remember a time soon after I had graduated from seminary in 1997 with my PhD. I was reading in my Bible one day and read this verse in Luke 16:15: "You are those who justify yourselves in the sight of men, but God knows your hearts; for that which is highly esteemed among men is detestable in the sight of God." I had just spent ten years in graduate school and completed the highest academic achievement possible. I was feeling pretty good about myself and was sure that my accomplishment was worthy of respect in the eyes of others. Then I read this verse. I heard the Lord saying that the things that men highly esteem are actually detestable in the sight of God. This does not mean that God hates education. He was the one who had told me to study and finish my degree. He was trying to show me a deeper truth. I saw that man is so susceptible in his flesh to hold things in high esteem. But God does not see things as man sees them. I struggled with this truth and questioned the Lord about how it was possible to suffer the loss of things in my life that were intangible.

The Lord helped me to see that I could never remove my PhD from my experience and reverse all the learning that I had done. I could not do that any more than Paul could stop being a Hebrew, or not be from the tribe of Benjamin, etc. I realized, however, that I could choose to consider it all loss for the sake of knowing Christ Jesus. I could suffer the loss of things like my reputation, education, nationality, and accomplishments just like Paul did. It is not about physically removing these things from our lives. It is all about letting go and not allowing these things to hold a place in our hearts. When I saw how my heart clung to those things for my own identity and for the praise of man, I understood what it meant to suffer the loss of those things for the sake of Christ.

Only Jesus wants to stand in the position of value and worth in your heart. Nothing you have ever accomplished or gained in this life can compare with knowing Him more and allowing Him to have His rightful place in your life. I can assure you that when you are willing to let go and suffer the loss of the things in your heart that compete with Jesus, there is a very real suffering that will take place. But it is worth it all to gain Him!

Since suffering is such an essential part of our Christian life, it is helpful to know how we should respond to it and what it is accomplishing. These two really go hand in hand, and the biblical writers make it very clear.

Read these verses and listen to the heart of men who had come to a proper understanding of the role suffering played in their lives.

- Now I rejoice in my sufferings for your sake, and in my flesh I do my share on behalf of His body, which is the church, in filling up what is lacking in Christ's afflictions (Col. 1:24).

- And not only this, but we also exult in our tribulations, knowing that tribulation brings about perseverance; and perseverance, proven character; and proven character, hope; and hope does not disappoint, because the love of God has been poured out within our hearts through the Holy Spirit who was given to us (Rom. 5:3-5).

- Consider it all joy, my brethren, when you encounter various trials, knowing that the testing of your faith produces endurance (James 1:2-3).

- In this you greatly rejoice, even though now for a little while, if necessary, you have been distressed by various trials (1 Peter 1:6).

The common thread in all these verses is our attitude toward suffering. We are to rejoice in our suffering! We rejoice because we know our suffering is directly connected to the same experiences that Jesus went through, and we are called for this purpose also since Jesus left us an example to follow in His steps (1 Peter 2:21).

We also have the assurance that our suffering is actually accomplishing something of great value in our lives. Paul called it a "glory that is to be revealed" (Rom. 8:18). He said, "For momentary, light affliction is producing for us an eternal weight of glory far beyond all comparison" (2 Cor. 4:17). This gives us hope that our suffering is never in vain.

There are a couple of important things to notice in these verses. First, the affliction we go through is "momentary" and "light," but the glory is "eternal" and has "weight." This means that whatever hardship we go through lasts only for a short time compared to eternity. It is also something that is actually "light" compared to the "weight" of the glory. This diagram gives us a visual to see this truth.

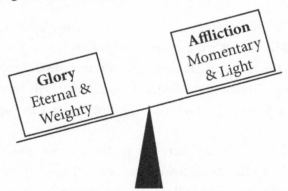

Second, the affliction "is producing" the glory. This means there is a direct relationship between the suffering and the glory. The glory is only possible if there is suffering. The suffering accomplishes something in our lives that only suffering can. This is why the Scriptures encourage us so specifically to see suffering as a normal part of life and to not despise the role it plays.

Suffering also has the purpose of bringing us into a deeper measure of fullness and maturity. Jesus "learned obedience from the things which He suffered" (Heb. 5:8), and

> ... it was fitting for Him, for whom are all things, and through whom are all things, in bringing many sons to glory, to perfect the author of their salvation through sufferings (Heb. 2:10).

Jesus needed to suffer so that He could learn obedience and be perfected. This may seem really hard to understand. It does not mean that Jesus was imperfect as though He had sin or moral imperfection. It means that there was a completion and bringing to fullness of all that God wanted to accomplish in and through Jesus' life that was only possible through Him suffering and learning to obey the Father even when it was hard.

The word "perfect" in this verse means "to complete" or "to fulfill." There were many things that needed to come to completion in Jesus' life, and this was not possible apart from suffering. This process reached its climax in His life when He told the Father, "...not My will, but Yours be done" (Luke 22:42).

In the same way, there are things in your life that must come to completion, and these will only happen through your suffering. God will use the hard things you experience to teach you obedience and bring you to a deeper place of fullness. This is the process of you knowing the "fellowship of His sufferings" (Phil. 3:10) and "filling up what is lacking in Christ's afflictions" (Col. 1:24). When you see this truth and embrace it by faith, you can grow in your ability to endure hardship, knowing that it is producing something in your life that is worth it all. This attitude is a sure sign of spiritual maturity and the mark of an obedient son or daughter.

Suffering connects you to the life of Jesus in the deepest and most intimate way. This is perhaps the most significant truth about suffering. As you experience suffering, you are literally touching the life of Jesus because He is present with you in your suffering. This is what Paul meant when he said he wanted to "know Him and the power of His resurrection and the fellowship of His sufferings" (Phil. 3:10). The word "fellowship" means intimate participation. When you suffer, Jesus is with you in your suffering. He chooses to fellowship with you in that most personal place in your life. The more you understand this mystical reality, the more you will understand the value of suffering. There is a depth of fellowship with Jesus that only happens when you suffer. This is why suffering is such a life-giving and essential truth.

Encountering the Truth

Truth: Suffering is part of being a Christian and God uses it in your life in ways that will teach you to depend on Him more, and it will produce an eternal glory that is far greater than your suffering now.

Faith Declaration: I will not resist or despise suffering in my life and will believe that I have the privilege to suffer with Jesus and to experience the fruitful benefits that will come as the result of suffering.

Walking in the Truth

Begin to see that suffering is a necessary part of your life as a child of God. Acknowledge that, while suffering is not pleasant, you want to experience intimacy and fellowship with Jesus in whatever suffering might come into your life. Believe the truth that your suffering is producing something in your life that you cannot always see or feel now. Be encouraged, knowing that Jesus is always with you in your suffering because your suffering is part of His suffering. Know that God will sustain you through whatever suffering you might experience and will bring you through it having a deeper intimacy with Him.

12

REST

So there remains a Sabbath rest for the people of God. For the one who has entered His rest has himself also rested from his works, as God did from His.

~ Hebrews 4:9-10

"Come to Me, all who are weary and heavy-laden, and I will give you rest. Take My yoke upon you and learn from me, for I am gentle and humble in heart, and you will find rest for your souls. For My yoke is easy and My burden is light."

~ Matthew 11:28-30

Have you ever felt "tired" in your Christian journey? There are many reasons that we experience being tired in the physical realm, but we can also become tired in our experience of the Christian life. Many people feel like being a Christian is hard and struggle to realize a sense of well-being and peace. I am convinced that a lot of this is because they have not been set free through the essential truth that I am sharing in this book. I have lived long enough to know that our sense of well-being does not come from our circumstances. It can only come from a deep-rooted knowledge of who we are as God's children and walking in the reality of all that He has done for us through Jesus Christ. This is why Jesus told us to come to Him to receive rest. Let's finish our journey together by looking at why rest is also an essential truth.

God knows that we need rest and He knows why. We have seen over and over that the decision the first man and woman made to disobey God had huge implications for the entire human race. Their actions literally reoriented how they lived, and subsequently how every person since then has ever lived. Before their rebellion, they enjoyed a perfect relationship with God and He supplied all they needed. After their rebellion, they lost their relationship with God and were left alone to provide for themselves, not only physically, but emotionally and mentally. Their relationship with God was broken and they were all alone to figure out how to live. Can you imagine the immensity of this experience?

As we seek to understand the true meaning of rest, let's consider one more time another difference between the Old Covenant and the New Covenant. God's first gesture to mankind to give him rest again was when He gave the Sabbath to the children of Israel as part of the Old Covenant. The notion of the Sabbath as a certain day of the week was so deeply rooted in the Hebrew understanding it was nearly impossible for the Jews during Jesus' day to think of it in any other way. This perception of rest being a specific day has significantly influenced our understanding also and given us a very limited view of the Sabbath. It is more than simply one day a week when we stop working and dedicate ourselves to the Lord. A day like this is beneficial and indeed probably a good practical suggestion, but it does not touch us deeply in our inner being where we long for rest. Before I explain the significance of the rest we find in Jesus, I want to first point out that Jesus is not only the fulfillment of the Sabbath—He fulfills all the details of the Old Covenant.

We have seen throughout this book that all of God's intentions are realized in and through Jesus Christ. The Sabbath, like all the other aspects of the Old Covenant, was just a shadow of something that would find its ultimate expression in the person of Jesus. This is what Paul meant when he said,

> Therefore no one is to act as your judge in regard to food or drink or in respect to a festival or a new moon or a Sabbath day—things which are a mere shadow of what is to come; but the substance belongs to Christ (Col. 2:16-17).

We see this throughout the history of the Jewish people. For example, Moses was the greatest leader among the Hebrews. He spoke face to face with God and received the law that God gave the Israelites in the wilderness. However, Moses told the Hebrews, "The Lord your God will raise up for you a prophet like me from among you, from your countrymen, you shall listen to him" (Deut. 18:15). Then the

Apostle Peter told us in Acts 3 that this prophet was Jesus and that "every soul that does not heed that prophet shall be utterly destroyed from among the people" (Acts 3:23). Moses saw clearly that his ministry to the Hebrew people was only a shadow that would find its ultimate expression in the ministry of Jesus (see also Heb. 3:1-6).

The blood of the Old Covenant passover lamb is another example of this foreshadowing. It was a preparation to help the Jews recognize Jesus as the sacrificial lamb. God instructed the children of Israel to apply the blood of the lamb to the doorposts of their homes during that first passover night in Egypt. After their deliverance from Egypt they observed the Passover meal as a memorial for what God had done for them, and it became a generational practice under the Old Covenant. But it was never meant to be a permanent practice. The sprinkling of the blood of animals was only a pattern of the great and final sacrifice that would take place on the cross. Jesus was "the lamb of God" (John 1:29, 36) and "our Passover" (1 Cor. 5:7) who became the final and complete sacrifice. "Through His own blood, He entered the holy place once for all, having obtained eternal redemption" (Heb. 9:12).

The priesthood of the Old Covenant was only a form of the more complete and better priesthood that was realized through the life of Jesus. He was not a descendant from the tribe of Levi, but of the tribe of Judah. This was a tribe that had nothing to do with priests. Despite this, we know that "according to the power of an indestructible life" (Heb. 7:16) Jesus was declared "a priest forever according to the order of Melchizedek" (Heb. 7:17).

Jesus even spoke of His own body as the replacement of the temple when He said, "Destroy this temple, and in three days I will raise it up" (John 2:19). The temple represented the very essence of Jewish life—religiously, culturally, and socially. Jesus referring to His body as the temple was one of the most significant statements He could make to the Jews.

These are all direct examples of fulfillment that took place in Jesus. There are also many other examples where Jesus was already the substance even during the time of the Old Covenant. For example, God fed the children of Israel for forty years in the desert with manna that fell from the sky every morning. Later Jesus told the Pharisees, "I am the bread that came down out of heaven" (John 6:41). Jesus took this truth to its ultimate application when He said, "My flesh is true food, and My blood is true drink. He who eats My flesh and drinks My blood abides in Me, and I in him" (John 6:55-56).

Jesus was not only the fulfillment, but the very essence of all that took place in the Old Covenant. Without a personal revelation of the significance of Jesus in all things, we cannot understand and live in the full reality of what God has for us as His children. Any attempt to interpret things outside of the life of Jesus Christ will always lead to an empty application devoid of the true substance—Jesus!

The Sabbath is a perfect example of an Old Covenant reality which finds its ultimate fulfillment in Jesus Christ. The history of the children of Israel shows us, while they may have faithfully observed a day called the Sabbath, they never entered into the Lord's rest. The psalmist told us that because of the rebellion in their hearts and their unbelief, God swore in His anger, "...they shall not enter into My rest" (Psalm 95:11). The writer of Hebrews confirmed this truth that the psalmist spoke hundreds of years earlier (Heb. 4:1-12). It shows us that true rest isn't just about not working on a specific day, it's about the condition of our heart. When it comes to rest, Jesus was more concerned about the greater reality than just a specific day. In the same way that Jesus is our righteousness, our life, and our purpose—He is our Sabbath!

Jesus said,

> "Come to Me, all who are weary and heavy-laden, and I will give you rest. Take My yoke upon you and learn from Me, for I am gentle and humble in heart, and you will find rest for your souls. For My yoke is easy and My burden is light" (Matthew 11:28-30).

The fact that Jesus offers to give us rest for our souls highlights the core issue. It is the problem that man has faced ever since the fall in the garden of Eden. The problem is that living life from our own strength and effort produces an immense burden upon our souls. Jesus promised that if we would come to Him, we would find rest for our souls. The rest that we need is not a physical rest for our bodies. Instead, we long for the rest that causes us to experience peace and contentment in our minds and emotions.

There are two reasons why we need rest for our souls. The first is because before we come to Jesus we have no assurance of being in a right relationship with God. We have already seen clearly that God has done everything necessary for us to receive the gift of life in Christ which fulfills our need for right standing before God. This brings peace and rest for our souls (Rom. 5:1-2).

The second reason we need rest for our souls is because living life independent from God makes us tired! We were not created to live from our own resources and self-effort. This is a very hard truth for many people to hear, especially in a modern world that promotes strength, independence, and self-reliance. But living in this way only produces striving, exhaustion, and weariness in our souls. This is why Jesus came to rescue us and teach us a new way of living. God's desire is to give us His life. We trust Him to live in us and through us. His yoke is easy and His burden is light. He promised that if we will come to Him, He will give us rest for our souls. Jesus understood that it was our souls that need rest, not just our bodies.

The writer of Hebrews brings all of this together for us in Hebrews 4. He encouraged his readers to not "come short" of the rest (Heb. 4:1) and that they should be "diligent" to enter the rest (Heb. 4:11). This means we should be eager and make every effort to enter the rest. He used the children of Israel as the example not to follow. The reason why they failed to enter God's rest was because they failed to unite their faith with God's word (Heb. 4:2). This is a crucial point for us to see. We must be willing to exercise our faith—believe and trust—in what God is telling us so that we can enter into His rest. If we don't have faith, we will miss it.

The writer of Hebrews connects rest to the creation story in which God rested on the seventh day. This is a very interesting thought. On the final day of His working, the sixth day, God created man and woman. The creation of

man and woman was the crowning touch on all that God
had created during that period of six days of work. The Bible
then tells us, "God rested on the seventh day from all His
works" (Gen. 2:2; Heb. 4:4). On the very next day after God
created man, He rested. This means that man's very first full
day of life was a day of rest with God! This highlights what
I believe to be an important—and often overlooked—truth.
God created us to live from a place of rest, not a place of
activity and work. We will surely be active in life, but that is
not the primary reason why God created us. Many of us live
in a place of perpetual activity and work in continual need
for rest. However, the truth is we need to live in the rest,
actively work, then return to the rest. As we do this, we work
from a place of rest, instead of resting as a result of work.
It may sound like a semantical difference, but getting God's
perspective on rest will revolutionize the way we live life.

Jesus came to bring you back to dependence and rest. You
have the opportunity to enter that rest in Him. The deepest
peace comes when you believe the truth of all that God has
done for you in Christ. He is your rest, and as you abide
in Him you are secure in your relationship with God. You
can rely on Him, knowing that He has provided everything
necessary for you to live life in Him to the fullest (2 Peter
1:3). Know and believe that God's acceptance is based on all
that Christ has done for you. This is where the invitation of
Jesus becomes a practical reality in your life. He wants you to
come to Him on a daily basis and enter into His rest.

🧠 Encountering the Truth

Truth: Jesus is your place of continual and lasting rest. He
is your Sabbath!

Faith Declaration: I no longer only recognize a certain time or place to rest because that idea is only a shadow of what God has promised me in Christ. The substance belongs to Jesus and I enter into Him and find total rest for my soul.

⚶ *Walking in the Truth*

Begin each day by aligning yourself with this wonderful truth. Recognize that Jesus is your rest, even when you are busy and active. He has invited you to come to Him and take His yoke. Realize that the other yokes you carry are heavy and burdensome. They cause you to feel tired and weary in your soul. Jesus' yoke is easy and light. When you wear His yoke, you do not have to perform for His approval and acceptance. As you know more deeply who He is and all that He has done for you, you can live completely free in Him, and He will give you rest for your soul!

CONCLUSION

I want to close with a synthesis of the essential truth that I have addressed by offering a personal "diary" of how I integrate this truth into my daily relationship with the Lord. This is my own process of how I affirm the truth in my life after many years of walking with the Lord. This truth has shaped my beliefs and impacted me at the deepest level possible.

I hope and pray that as you read this conclusion you will see how the Lord wants the truth to set you free at a deeper level as well. You may even want to use this as a tool in your devotional time to read and confess the truth over your own life; or you may want to rewrite it and make it more personal as you experience the truth setting you free.

Thank you again for taking the time to read this book. I trust you have been blessed and encouraged in your own personal journey with the Lord.

How I Live My Life According to the Essential Truth

I have a deep and abiding belief and conviction that God has an all-encompassing and ultimate **purpose**. He will accomplish this purpose through His Son, Jesus Christ. God determined before He ever created anything that this purpose would be the path that He follows throughout all of time and eternity. When He created man and woman, He created them for the sole intent to have loving fellowship and union by sharing His life with them. When man declared his independence from God by his disobedience in the garden of Eden, God began a process of events that manifested throughout history to bring us back again to the place of perfect fellowship and union with Him. This was finally accomplished by God sending His Son, Jesus Christ, to earth to live as a man and model for us what it means to live a life fully dependent upon God the Father for everything.

I have been called by God according to His eternal purpose in Christ Jesus. This purpose is what determines all that God does in my life on a daily basis. He wants me to be exactly like His Son—Jesus Christ. He is using everything that I experience in life to conform me to the image of Jesus. As I live my life, I live with the awareness that this is what God is doing continually.

My **perspective** has completely changed since I have come to understand—by the revelation of the Spirit in my life—that in Christ I am a new creation. I have a completely new nature. I am part of the new man in Christ, and this man is righteous and holy. My personal righteousness is real and true. It is not something that is theological or only positional. God has placed me in Christ. Because I am in Christ, Christ makes me holy, righteous, and beyond reproach. God will not find fault with me. This brings a deep sense of security and joy in my life. Because I am a spiritual person now, I have the capacity to see things as God sees them. Living my life from God's perspective changes the way I experience every aspect of my life.

I am aware that the **grace** of God has been given to me through the life of Jesus. His grace empowers me to partake in God's life and to live my life in Him. I do not live my life in my own strength and effort, but only by grace, which is the very presence of Jesus in me.

I believe by **faith** and trust completely that Christ lives in my body by the presence of His Spirit which He has given me. I believe that Christ is the essence of my life and decide every day that He will live in me, through me, as me as I trust in Him to do so. He is more than able to live His life in me as His vessel. The more I believe this truth and submit myself to Him, He transforms my life into His image.

I know that because of my faith in God, He has made me completely righteous. This means that I am in perfect standing with God and there is nothing I have to do to earn His approval or meet His demands. I have become the **righteousness** of God in Christ Jesus. God is pleased with me, and I can live in total assurance that I am accepted and loved at all times.

When the Holy Spirit revealed to me that I was a sinner and needed to confess my sins before God and accept the free gift of God in Christ Jesus by faith, I chose to believe and put my trust in Him. When I did this, I received God's **forgiveness** for all of my sins—past, present, and future. I know with full conviction that since that time all of my sins are forgiven. I never wonder if God will forgive me. If I ever do anything sinful, He has already forgiven me, and all I need to do is live in the awareness of His forgiveness that was secured through the shed blood of Jesus.

I do not live with a sin-conscience anymore because I know that the blood of Jesus has washed my conscious clean.

I do not have to keep track of my sins anymore because they have been forgiven and God has chosen to remember them no more. As God's child, I do not have to practice **confession** in order to receive God's forgiveness. I do not hope that God will forgive me, nor do I have to live in fear that if I do not confess my sins to Him He will not forgive me. I know that He forgave me once and for all when Jesus died on the cross, and that I experienced His forgiveness personally when I first believed in Him. There is no cause and effect relationship between confession and forgiveness in my life because that would mean that the blood of Jesus was not sufficient enough for God and that my confession would be a necessary work. This would negate faith and undermine the very essence of the gospel.

I believe that I have personally experienced the crucifixion, death, burial, and resurrection of Jesus. This happened because I was in Christ when He experienced these things. Whatever Christ experienced, I experienced. Though it is a mystery, it is not for this reason any less true or real. Since I died with Christ, I died to **Sin** once and for all. Sin no longer has any power over my life. I have died to Sin, and I am now alive to God in Christ Jesus. The working activity of the life of Jesus in me has set me free from the principle of Sin and death that used to operate in my life. This means that I am free from Sin!

For the remainder of my days on earth I will have the experience of living in my natural body. In this natural condition, the **flesh** is still present in me. This is the area of my life where I have the potential to do the things I do not want to do. But God has provided me with His Spirit—as well as the abundance of His grace—and as long as I choose to walk in the Spirit, I will not fulfill the desire of the flesh. When I recognize any area of my life that comes from the flesh, I can, by faith, practically take that area to the cross and crucify it so that it no longer has a place in my life.

I know that the **Spirit** of Christ, which is the Spirit of God, dwells in me. His Spirit constantly testifies to me that I am His child. His Spirit teaches me all I need to know about God and leads me into all the truth that is in Christ Jesus. The Spirit, which raised Jesus from the dead, also gives life to my mortal body in order to manifest the life of Christ through me every day.

I realize that in this life I will go through **suffering**. I believe that Jesus is with me during these times. Not only is He with me, but He is actively working and causing my suffering to have great value. I may not be able to see it now or ever in this life, but I fully believe there is an eternal glory that my suffering is producing for me. I know Christ more intimately through all the things that I suffer. I also choose to suffer the loss of all things in my own life so that I may gain Christ. I make the decision to not put my identity in my strengths and accomplishments and desire only to know Jesus more.

All of this truth points to everything God has done for me in Christ so that I can stop striving and experience His **rest** and peace. When I know and believe the truth in my inner being, Jesus leads me in His rest. This rest causes me to be at peace with myself, God, and others around me. It is a profound knowing that God is deeply pleased with me and that I am His beloved child.

I know that God has fully succeeded in doing everything that was necessary to accomplish His desire to restore me to perfect fellowship and union with Him through His Son, Jesus Christ.

The *Essential Truth* defines my life and I live with this constant awareness every day. As one who has fully embraced the truth, I live as a Christian. I pray regularly. I read the Scriptures. I share my faith with others as the Lord gives me opportunity. I give. I trust God. I fellowship with other believers. I practice spiritual gifts and much, much more. These are all the natural expressions of the life of Christ that is within me, but they do not determine my identity. Whether I do them a lot, a little, or not at all, cannot ever change the truth of what God has done for me in Christ Jesus.

I know the truth and the truth has set me free!

BENEDICTION

A benediction is the pronouncement of a blessing. It is often given at the conclusion of a church service. The writers of the New Testament also wrote benedictions at the end of many of their letters to the churches.

My most meaningful experience of the benediction was when I was in seminary. One of my professors, Dr. E. Earle Ellis, often pronounced a benediction when he finished his lecture. Dr. Ellis was a most unique and peculiar man. He was single his entire life and was fully devoted to his academic studies. As a world-class theologian, he made a significant contribution to Pauline studies as well as writing commentaries on various books of the New Testament. He lived in a personal retro world of plaid polyester pants, wide-collared shirts, and skinny leather neck ties.

Stephanie and I had the privilege of developing a personal relationship with Dr. Ellis and hosted him in our home on numerous occasions. During these personal interactions, Dr. Ellis would passionately share the convictions of his personal devotion to the Lord Jesus. His life of study, steeped deeply in the Scriptures, manifested in a profound knowledge of the Lord that inspired my life as a young and hungry student.

At the end of his lectures, Dr. Ellis would close his notes and ask us to stand to our feet. Stretching out his lanky arms graciously towards us with his hands extended and palms open, he would speak beautiful words of blessing upon our lives from his heart and from the Scriptures. With tears in his eyes, he would complete his benediction and promptly exit the room to return to his mysterious life as a theological recluse. Dr. Ellis deeply impacted me and planted seeds of understanding that have grown into maturity over the past thirty years.

In honor of Dr. Ellis, who is now in the presence of Jesus, I extend a benediction over your life.

Now may the God of peace, who brought up from the dead the great Shepherd of the sheep through the blood of the eternal covenant, even Jesus our Lord, equip you in every good thing to do His will, working in you that which is pleasing in His sight, through Jesus Christ. May He establish you deeply and firmly in the true knowledge of His Son, and empower you to walk in the reality of all the truth in Him, and preserve you faithful until the very end. May the Lord bless you and keep you. May He make His face shine on you and be gracious to you. May the Lord lift up His countenance on you and give you peace. To Him be the glory forever and ever. Amen. (Heb. 13:20-21; Col. 3:10; 2 Peter 1:8; Num. 6:24-26).

Recommended Reading

This is a short list of books that have been extremely helpful to me in my personal journey. I would not consider myself a prolific reader. In fact, I am very discriminating about what I do read. These books are those that have significantly impacted me personally. I am sure there are many more books that would do the same if I were to take the time to read them.

Some of these books below are out of print, but I believe you can buy most of them on the Internet. Also, some relate directly to the content of this present book, while others address topics that fall outside of the scope of this book.

Boyd, Gregory. *Cross Vision: How the Crucifixion of Jesus Makes Sense of Old Testament Violence.* Minneapolis, MN: Fortress Press, 2017.

Boyd, Gregory. *The Crucifixion of the Warrior God.* Minneapolis, MN: Fortress Press, 2017.

Chambers, Oswald. *My Utmost for His Highest.* Grand Rapids, MI: Discovery House Publishers, 2010.

Eger, Edith. *The Choice.* New York, NY: Scribner Press, 2018.

Edwards, Gene. *Climb the Highest Mountain*. Jacksonville, FL: SeedSowers, 1984.

Fowler, James A. *The Extent and Efficacy of the Life and Work of Jesus Christ*. Fallbrook, CA: C.I.Y. Publishing, 2013.

Frankl, Viktor. *Man's Search for Meaning*. Boston, MA: Beacon Press, 2006.

Fromke, DeVern. *No Other Foundation*. Cloverdale, IN: Sure Foundation, 1965.

Fromke, DeVern. *Ultimate Intention*. Pickle Partners Publishing, 1962.

Fromke, DeVern. *Unto Full Stature*. Knoxville, TN: Sure Foundation, 2001.

Laird, Martin. *Into the Silent Land*. New York, NY: Oxford University Press, 2006.

Nee, Watchman. *The Normal Christian Life*. Bombay, India: Gospel Literature Service, 1957.

Nouwen, Henri J.M. *The Spirituality of Fundraising*. Nashville, TN: Upper Room Books, 2011.

Scazzero, Peter. *Emotionally Healthy Spirituality*. Grand Rapids, MI: Zondervan, 2006.

Sparks, T. Austin. *Prophetic Ministry*. Shoals, IN: Old Paths Tract Society, Inc., 1989.

Stone, Dan and Gregory, David. *The Rest of the Gospel: When the Partial Gospel Has Worn You Out*. Eugene, OR: Harvest House Publishers, 2014.

INDEX OF SCRIPTURES

To order additional copies of

ESSENTIAL
TRUTH

contact us at info@equipperssa.com

or visit our website at www.equipperssa.com.

Quantity discounts are available for orders over five books.

Made in the USA
Coppell, TX
04 March 2022

74443057R00114